LOVE LOCK

Place me like a seal over your heart, like a seal on your arm; for love is as strong as death.
(Song of Songs 8:6)

LOVE LOCK

CREATING LASTING CONNECTIONS
WITH THE ONE YOU LOVE

Rich Rollins, DMin
and
Marty Trammell, PhD

Authors of *Redeeming Relationships: How to Resolve
10 Common Conflicts (and reduce their frequency!)* and
Spiritual Fitness: A Guide to Biblical maturity

CrossLink Publishing

CrossLink Publishing
1601 Mt. Rushmore Rd, Ste 3288
Rapid City, SD 57701
www.crosslinkpublishing.com

Ordering Information:
Quantity sales. Special discounts are available on quantity purchases by corporations, associations, and others. For details, contact the "Special Sales Department" at the address above.

Love Lock/Rollins & Trammell —1st ed.

ISBN 978-1-63357-158-7
Library of Congress Control Number: 2018952675
First edition: 10 9 8 7 6 5 4 3 2 1

Unless otherwise noted, all scripture quotations are taken from THE HOLY BIBLE, NEW INTERNATIONAL VERSION®, NIV® Copyright © 1973, 1978, 1984, 2011 by Biblica, Inc.® Used by permission. All rights reserved worldwide.

Scripture quotations marked "ESV" are taken from The Holy Bible, English Standard Version. Copyright © 2000; 2001 by Crossway Bibles, a division of Good News Publishers. Used by permission. All rights reserved.

Note: Many stories in this book are composites of real-life experiences. In other cases, the authors have changed individuals' names. When they share their own experiences, their names appear at the beginning in parentheses.

To LouAnna Rollins and Linda Trammell:
your love, laughter, forgiveness, and faith
have continued to offer us a love that
is both "more delightful than wine"
and "as strong as death"
(Song of Songs 1:2; 8:6).

MIRIAM, FOR BEING
THANKS FOR BEING
AN INSPIRING STUDENT
AND CHRISTIAN SISTER

Contents

Acknowledgments...1

As We Begin 3

We Love for Reasons 5

I Need to Feel Understood

Chapter 1: Playing in the Same Key.............................. 13

Chapter 2: Cherishing Differences 19

Chapter 3: Listening Your Way to Love......................... 27

I Need to Feel Valued

Chapter 4: The Magic in a Kiss.................................... 35

Chapter 5: Editing Expectations 41

Chapter 6: Shelving Expectations 49

Chapter 7: Tracking Storms 57

I Need to Feel a Part of You

Chapter 8: Promoting Partnership................................ 67

Chapter 9: One + One = One?..................................... 75

Chapter 10: Defining Definitions................................. 81

I Need to Feel Appreciated and Cherished

Chapter 11: Taking the Medicine.................................. 91

Chapter 12: Maturity Matters...................................... 97

I Need to Trust You

Chapter 13: Dealing with Damaged Trust 105

Chapter 14: Come Out of the Cold!............................ 111

I Need More Resolution, Less Conflict

Chapter 15: Shruggers 121

Chapter 16: The War of Two Worlds........................... 127

Chapter 17: Get Invited!.. 135

Chapter 18: Contentment's Kiss 141

All God's Best! 147

About the Authors 149

Acknowledgments

Special thanks (from Rich) to:

My wife, LouAnna, and my parents, who have always modeled a strong love.

My friend and writing partner, Marty, whose authentic Christianity and infectious
love for others have modeled Jesus to me.

My daughters and sons-in-law, whose encouragement and presence in my life has
made a difference.

Our foster daughters, who have reminded us daily of the importance of being Jesus in the lives of those around us.

Our circle of Long Beach friends, whose generosity, love, and fellowship has
enriched our lives.

Special thanks (from Marty) to:

My wife and best friend, Linda, whose strong and tender love continues to reflect Jesus Christ to the world and sprinkle stardust on our dreams!

My mom and recently departed dad, for doing the hard work together.

My sons and daughters-in-law, whose maturing love deeply reflects the Father's.

My friend and writing partner, Rich, whose generous and joyful spirit continues to help me understand the Father's love.

My lifetime friend and writing consultant, David Sanford, whose daily prayers and wisdom encouraged not only this writing ministry but my entire life.

My pastors: James Godwin, Donn Mogford, David Miller, Tom Younger, and Greg Trull, whose commitment to the Scriptures inspired many of these pages.

My family: The Trammells, Markwoods, Farwells, and Hansens who put up with my many meanderings and prayed this book through.

My students and friends at Corban and Perrydale whose stories fill these pages.

My heavenly Father, whose love for me is, conclusively, "stronger than death."

Special thanks (from both of us) to:

David Sanford, whose wise and cheerful advice made this book, and the work that went into it, so much more meaningful.

Our publisher, Rick Bates, our excellent editor, Ashley Casteel, and the others at CrossLink Publishing, whose belief in these pages and professional experience printed our hopes and our hearts.

Our special friends whose hospitality made this book possible: Mark and Connie Hawkins, Floyd and Jeannette Votaw, and Berniece Rollins.

Our special friends who believed in this book and had the courage to share their love stories with candor and frankness.

Most of all, we thank the Author of love Himself. May we experience and promote the enduring love He desires for us all.
—Rich and Marty

As We Begin . . .

"Set me as a seal upon your heart,
as a a seal upon your arm,
for love is strong as death,
jealousy is fierce as the grave.
Its flashes are flashes of fire,
the very flame of the Lord.
Many waters cannot quench love,
neither can floods drown it.
If a man offered for love
all the wealth of his house,
he would be utterly despised" (ESV).
Song of Songs 8:6–7

We hope these chapters will encourage the "strengthening" of your love so that you will be able to join the lovers in the Song of Songs and experience the connection that the best of love creates.

We Love for Reasons

"The reason my Father loves me is . . ."
John 10:17

In the *New York Times*, Mandy Len Catron wrote about how complete strangers fell in love during a social experiment in which they answered thirty-six questions and then stared into each other's eyes for four minutes. In "To Fall in Love With Anyone, Do This," Catron shares how she decided to attend one of the sessions herself with an acquaintance who she "didn't know particularly well." The result? She fell in love and married him.[1] Catron's article led to a TED Talk that went viral. During her presentation she explained how her initial skepticism about whether or not romantic love could be fabricated, turned into, well, belief in the power of manufactured love.

Why did Catron's personal discovery attract so much attention? Should it surprise us that intense listening and prolonged eye contact increase romantic feelings? It's easy to forget that there are *reasons* that love's magic works. Jesus pointed this out to several religious leaders when He reminded them that simply belonging to God wasn't enough. He said that the Father loved Him, the Son, not because He was a descendant of Abraham, not because He was part of the trinity, but because, within His unconditional love, God loves "for reasons."

---

1. Mandy Len Catron, "To Fall in Love With Anyone, Do This," *New York Times*, January 9, 2015, https://www.nytimes.com/2015/01/11/fashion/modern-love-to-fall-in-love-with-anyone-do-this.html.

Because our Father created us in His image, our marriages improve when we accept the premise that, like our Father, our spouses love *for reasons*. Rich and I have found that in marriage counseling, the couples who struggle the most are often those who expect the most. Expecting unconditional love without providing reasons to be loved contradicts creation. This contradiction can promote disillusionment and dissatisfaction—emotional conditions the enemy uses to damage the delight God longs to give us.

*The couples who struggle most are
often those who expect the most.*

Part of the wisdom of the Song of Songs shows up in the *reasons* the husband and wife provide each other. These "reasons" grow the vineyard of their love and promote the dances and delights they regularly enjoy as a married couple. It is clear from the arias they sing that their romance is far deeper than unconditional love—like their Father in heaven, Lady Wisdom and her husband love for reasons.

*"The reason my Father loves me
is that I lay down my life."*
John 10:17

*"Greater love has no one than this, that
he lay down his life for his friends."*
John 15:13

Jesus explained to the religious leaders that laying down our lives for each other adds another dimension to the unconditional love we experience—just as Jesus's sacrifice deepened our experience of the love of the Father. In marriage, this analogous laying down of our lives deepens the friendship we share.

An Example from the Song of Songs

My own vineyard I have neglected.
Song of Songs 1:6

Solomon's bride begins their marriage struggling with self-perception. Her low view of herself combined with the early date of this aria, make her a reluctant muse for many of the world's romantic laments – for the "ugly ducking" stories that fill the libraries of many young brides.

Solomon's wife, reminds us with the painful beauty of her song that our rebellion against God still breaks our hearts and blinds us to the beauty God sees. Her lyric "my own vineyard I have neglected" changes in the last chapter to "my own vineyard is mine to give." What causes her to move away from seeing herself as mostly broken to seeing herself as a blessing? What changes her song?

Love does. As the human representative of wisdom, Solomon, the wise husband, doesn't preach, and he doesn't interrupt her song or rewrite the melody. Instead, he changes the solo of her sadness into a duet. He enters her world, the feelings of her heart, and sings a harmony that fills her with hope. He expresses to her what he (and by poetic extension, God the Father) feels so deeply about her. Solomon *lays down* his life, sacrificing time and energy to write an aria that brilliantly responds to her discouragement. He sings about her beauty, comparing her to the stunning million-dollar mare he purchased from Egypt's pharaoh (Song of Songs 1:9). He *lays down* his life again, sacrificing part of their income and his time to involve others in the making of jewelry for her (v. 11). These offerings, brought to the altar of marriage, change the story of the ugly duckling into the song of the swan.

The realities of life in our Snapchatting, Twitter-obsessed culture make these sacrifices rare. We either forget to or are unwilling to make them—and that's a major difference between a marriage that feels like a song and, well, a relationship that feels like fugues modulating through minor keys. Solomon and his wife knew that everyone loves *for reasons*—that love can and should be manufactured.

Taking the time to write something romantic and healing for each other and spending time and money involving someone else in the making of a gift can heal the hurt and warm the cold communication climate breathed-out by the darkness around us.

Solomon's efforts to manufacture love foreshadow Paul's instructions to husbands: "Husbands, love your wives, just as Christ loved the church and gave himself up for her" (Ephesians 5:25).

Although none of our sacrifices compare to the sacrifice of the Son of God, they do promote similar emotional and spiritual connections and closeness. Jesus's words, "*The reason* my father loves me is that I *lay down my life*," remind us that when unconditional love strolls hand in hand with manufactured love, we enjoy the deeper intimacies the creator of love intended.

About This Book

When Brand Mountain Design proposed a cover design and the title *Love Lock* for this book, Rich and I thought, "Will readers know what that means?" But, when they shared with us the growing romantic trend for couples to fasten padlocks on bridges in Rome and Paris, and the research that suggests millennials and screenagers are searching for more permanent relationships, we knew it could work.

Although Paris and Rome have imposed fines because their historic bridges are being compromised by the weight of the locks, officials there are still finding it difficult to dissuade couples from the practice. Why? Because hanging locks on a bridge and throwing away the key symbolizes the hope that a stronger, more permanent, and more secure kind of relationship is possible. If it is still true that "what the world needs now is love," it is certainly this kind. The more Rich and I prayed, the more we realized the title was a good fit, because the love lock phenomenon also reflects humanity's deep, universal longing for connection and commitment—for a love that God describes as "stronger than death" (Song of Songs 8:6).

This book is our studied response to the needs we've observed in our combined sixty years of counseling, and it is our humble attempt to point out the Bible's answers to the growing loneliness and lack of connection documented in the research journals. We organized the content into sections that respond to the most common reasons couples self-report for seeking counseling:

- I need to feel understood.
- I need to feel valued.
- I need to feel a part of the one I love.
- I need to feel respected and cherished.
- I need to be able to trust the one I love.
- I need to experience more resolution and less conflict.

As you read through these pages, we believe you will find what others have already found—that we CAN experience a deeper connection, an honest human love that locks on to "the life that is truly life" (I Timothy 6:19).

Warmly, Rich and Marty

I Need to Feel Understood

*A so-called happy marriage corresponds to love
as a correct poem to an improvised song.*
—Karl Wilhelm Friedrich Schlegel

CHAPTER 1

Playing in the Same Key

When musicians play in different keys, the dissonance is painful. Only when an orchestra moves together from key to key—major to minor and minor to major—will its members experience the harmony and beauty of their music. Relationships work the same way.

Sitting at Starbucks, Kate and Stuart began to reflect on the results of their last counseling session. For the first time they began to see the major issues in their marriage as major issues and the minor issues as minor. They finally agreed that the counselor was right when she said that unless they could differentiate between major and minor issues, they would never develop the kind of communication climate that would help them fully understand each other.

Majoring on the Minor

Several years after graduating from college, I (Rich) worked as a medical technologist in a local hospital. I arrived one afternoon to an explosion of angry words coming from the outpatient waiting room. In the middle of the room stood the associate hospital administrator and my boss. Nose to nose they stood, name-calling, neither willing to back down. My gaze migrated to the patients shifting uncomfortably in the vinyl chairs. I remember feeling embarrassed for these two "adults."

The conflict involved the chair arrangement in the waiting room. The administrator felt it was his responsibility to determine the outpatient waiting room layout. My boss was determined not to relinquish any ground in the matter. Everyone except these two saw this as a minor issue. Sometime later my boss asked my opinion about the "discussion."

"If you expend that kind of energy over the placement of a few chairs, what kind of response will you have when the issue is a major one?" I asked. Disturbed that I didn't take her side in the matter, she tried to make the conflict more significant.

"What right does he have to come down here and dictate the arrangement of our outpatient room?" From my perspective, she had rationalized her outburst over a minor issue by trying to make the issue seem more important than it was. She had done little to demonstrate a desire to understand and support her colleague.

Several months later, the administration made some demands on our area that negatively affected our work. We had no lines of communication for resolving the situation since our boss was perceived by the administration as a "reactor." This time, her legitimate complaint was ignored because she had overreacted earlier to a problem she should have labeled "minor." The same is true in marriage—when we respond to a minor issue in a major way, we undermine our future ability to effectively resolve conflict and create the kind of friendship that encourages a deeper understanding.

Minoring on the Major

Just as it is never wise to treat a minor conflict as a major one, it isn't helpful to treat a major conflict as if it were minor. The Bible's dramatic love poem, the Song of Songs, describes the importance of making sure we take a serious look at conflicts in our marriages before we call them "minor." In a passage where the bride is hiding from her lover because she views herself as inadequate—as plain and ordinary—the lover warns, "Catch for us the foxes, the little foxes that ruin the vineyards, our vineyards that are in bloom" (Song of Songs 2:15).

The "little foxes" are things (like a person's view of his or her attractiveness) that, although they appear to be "little," can seriously ruin the delights (the "vineyards") in a relationship. Most of us would think that the large foxes would be a more serious threat, because they're large enough to eat the fruit and ruin the harvest. But the "little foxes" are actually the most dangerous because they eat at the root and destroy the entire vine. What Solomon seems to be telling us is that the intoxicating aspects (the "vineyards") in a marriage are damaged when we minor on the majors.

When my wife and I (Marty) cover this passage in premarital counseling, we usually find Solomon's point confirmed. Many women identify with the young bride in this ancient love story but fail to realize that how they feel about their beauty affects the harmony in their marriage.

Solomon's point is that women (and men) who treat their low opinion of their attractiveness as a minor conflict often find less intimacy and understanding in their marriages. The Lover's point is important to repeat: Make sure you catch the "little foxes," because the damage they do is major.

Rob discovered this the hard way.

> *"Pastor, Lynn just left me . . . she says*
> *she wants a divorce . . . she says*
> *she can't live this way anymore."*

Rob was devastated. He had arrived home from a business trip to find his house empty. His wife had left him a message on his phone. To make matters worse, Lynn had found another man who demonstrated a desire to understand her—her boss.

A pastor's every ounce of concern is poured into such calls. Now I (Rich) was being asked to fix a marriage that had been filled with unresolved conflict for years. After several calls, Lynn and Rob finally came into my office. Within a few minutes it became evident that for a decade, Lynn had been attempting to resolve some major conflicts that Rob saw as only minor. Although Rob began to see things from Lynn's perspective, the issues had escalated, and while resolution was still possible, it was not probable.

I wish I could report that Rob and Lynn are not Christians, but they are. I wish I could tell you that they acknowledged the discord in their marriage, but they didn't. I wish I could tell you that they confessed their parts in the conflicts and got back together, but I cannot. Lynn kept hoping that Rob would, "grab a clue" and Rob kept thinking the conflicts would "go away." Rob got his wish, but not in the way he had hoped.

Couples who make either of the mistakes we've written about here ("majoring on the minor" or "minoring on the major") create dissonance in their marriages. Successful marriages involve spouses who learn to ask regularly, "Are there issues I'm blowing out of proportion?" and "Are there major issues I'm treating as minor?"

Answering these kinds of questions and completing the "Love Lock" activity below can help you *feel understood* and loved for who you are. Couples who use their deepening understanding of each other to learn to play in the same key have a better chance of enjoying a lifetime of good music.

Love Lock: Playing in the Same Key

You're about to create some of your own "music," so turn off any media devices you have with you and follow these steps:

- On a blank piece of paper or a restaurant napkin, draw a clef (five parallel lines about an inch apart).

- On the top line of the left side of the clef, trace a quarter, nickel or dime (or just draw a circle).

- Take turns writing in the circle one word from one conversation you enjoyed (recent or long ago). Avoid any comments that might create dissonance!

- Repeat this two more times, moving from the left circle to the right side of the clef (for a total of three circles with three separate words from conversations you enjoyed).

- For the next few minutes, share how talking about these subjects makes you feel.

- Continue talking for as long as you want to, and then—well, that's up to you!

CHAPTER 2

Cherishing Differences

When LouAnna and I (Rich) first started dating, I thought I had found the person of my dreams. I had finally found a woman who would let me talk for the entire date. She would gaze into my eyes, smile, and nod as I pontificated about solutions to the problems of the world. Later she confessed that she was drawn to me because she was not expected to talk a lot. She had finally found someone who would carry the conversation and not require much feedback. I loved this trait, until we married and encountered our first conflict. I think out loud. LouAnna speaks only after thinking. When we encountered problems in our relationship, I wanted to talk about it right then!

The intensity I projected into the conflict caused LouAnna to retreat into silence. The more I demanded responses, the quieter she became. Over the years, we both have moved to the middle. I have learned the value of timing, and she has learned to respond even if she's not as ready as she'd like to be. We are all different. Our differences either strengthen or weaken our relationships.

Screeching Brakes

When people live together, their differences show up—usually unannounced. Day after day, they step off the curb and out into the traffic lanes of our lives. Screeching brakes and horns blaring, we're often frustrated by these unexpected intruders. Unless we can see how the "differences" complement our way of life, we find ourselves exasperated. And sometimes, even in our churches, it seems like there's no one who can help us. So we struggle on our own, trying to develop communication skills that signal a more mature relationship.

Some of the greatest differences we face come from our personalities. In their book, *Opposites Attack: Turning Your Differences into Opportunities*, Jack and Carole Mayhall list some of the personality differences that create conflict:

- Differences based on how we think: Factual vs. Intuitive, Logical vs. Relational
- Differences based on the way we relate: Introvert vs. Extrovert, Affectionate vs. Reserved
- Differences based on the way we talk: Revealer vs. Concealer
- Differences based on the way we act: Perfectionist vs. Non-Perfectionist, Aggressive vs. Timid
- Differences based on the way we look at life: Pessimistic vs. Optimistic[1]

Although some couples are initially drawn to each other because of differences in their personalities, after a while they discover that these same differences can divide the best of friends. When this happens in our marriages, we need to remember that God created many of our differences. The psalmist wrote:

For you created my inmost being; you knit me to-
gether in my mother's womb. I praise you because I
am fearfully and wonderfully made; your works are
wonderful. . . . All the days ordained for me were
written in your book before one of them came to be.
Psalm 139:13–14, 16.

Like the psalmist, we are born with "appointed" differences. Other differences, like habits, are added to our personalities by family, friends, and the entertainments we choose. When we work to cherish differences of either kind (those we're born with or those we pick up as we experience life) we reduce the potential for conflict. Most counselors will tell you that, after a few experiences of working through differences, it gets easier. And happily married couples will tell you that often the differences that seem most divisive are the very differences that draw them closest together. Whether our conflicts are related to differences such as how many lattes to buy in a week, how to initiate romance, how to perform a specific task in the home, or how to raise children, we can learn to deal with differences.

To write a chapter for a business textbook on how to teach conflict resolution, I (Marty) talked with other professionals and read hundreds of pages about helping employees work through their differences. Those ideas, along with the wisdom in Proverbs, helped us develop two simple questions we often use to reduce the number and severity of relational conflicts in our own lives. These same questions are in the material that we use during premarital and marriage counseling sessions.

1. Will spending time and energy on getting my spouse to change really be all that profitable? (If that worked, you probably wouldn't be reading this chapter, right?)

2. Is it possible that the difference I'm wrestling with may actually add some positive quality to my life and our marriage?

Mature people understand that it's not necessary for everyone to see everything the same way. If seen as strengths, our differences can actually help us walk the road toward more meaningful marriages. Here's an approach that can help us discover the value in our differences.

Think "Team"

God has made us unique, not for the purpose of driving each other nuts, but so that we can be stronger. For example, intuitive people need concrete thinkers around to remind them of the details and inspect and check records. Concrete thinkers can also help the intuitive personality remain calm and patient.

Concrete thinkers need intuitive dreamers to introduce ingenuity to their solutions, help them see the possibilities and potentials, and serve as cheerleaders when projects seem overwhelming. We need to think "team."

Do an Assessment

Do you know how you are wired? Take a personality test. It'll help you assess your personality type and evaluate how it affects your perspectives in life and in your marriage.

Take Control

You are the only person you can control. Backseat drivers are appreciated as much in relationships as they are on the interstate. Rather than trying to become the Holy Spirit in your marriage, become a detective. Ask questions about yourself, like, "In what way do *I* drive others nuts?" (The free "Spiritual Fitness" notes on our website, redeemingrelationships.com, can help once you reach this point.)

Connecting

Our family differences showed up at our wedding reception! Marie came from a conservative white family, so they served cake, punch, and mints. After returning from our honeymoon, we saw pictures of the party my Catholic, Mexican family threw after the reception. They had dancing, alcohol, and lots of food—and Marie's family was not invited!

Our advice? Try to celebrate differences—it can be so rewarding! But it takes communication, compromise, a willingness to see things from another viewpoint, and forgiveness. —Vic and Marie (married 51 years)

Give Permission and Listen

Early in my marriage I (Rich) gave my family and friends permission to tell me how my personality affected them. I thought there would be only a few conversations. However, I found them more frequent than I wanted. Most were on target! It's not that confrontation has no place in a marriage. The Scriptures teach about its importance within the local church (see Galatians 6:1). The problem is that too many of us begin to view our place in the marriage as equal with the role of the Holy Spirit. Instead of "giving" each other permission to confront, we are too eager to point out the faults within our spouse's personality. Giving permission to point out faults takes courage and humility—a humility that changes the nature and impact of the confrontation. Without permission, all but the boldest will avoid confronting us. We need to give people permission to confront us, and we need to listen honestly to their point of view. Such permission and listening can transform a marriage.

Be Candid

Be candid and frank about the impact personality differences make in your relationship. Too often we ignore them or we deny their impact, not wanting to appear weak, and wanting instead to remain in control, to appear stronger than we really are. Jesus taught us another way. He said that His strength comes to us in our weakness (2 Corinthians 12:9) and Paul, in talking about the churches, said, "When I am weak, then I am strong." (2 Corinthians 12:10). The principles of weakness, humility, and meekness are difficult to value in a culture that worships self-sufficiency, but they can help us with our differences. Admit them, study them, and take notes about how specific differences emotionally impact you. Share your notes with each other. Let your candid conversations about each difference inspire a new determination that can help you turn conflict into closeness.

Differences in personality and perspective don't have to divide our marriages. We can be honest about them and learn to allow those differences to create an ever-deepening oneness . A oneness that helps us find in our living the death of Christ—the one whose demonstration of love, despite our horrific differences, reunited the human race with its Creator. Learning to sacrifice our own perspectives can secure the depth of our love for our spouses. We have seen it again and again: trading the difficulties in our differences for a new determination is truly redemptive.

Love Lock: Cherishing Differences

- Using your phone, a restaurant napkin, or 3×5 card, list two differences between you and your spouse.

- Next to the two differences, write out two possible benefits the difference might bring to your friendship.

- Text or hand the list to your spouse.

- When you receive the list, add one more benefit your difference might bring to your marriage.

- Take a walk in a nearby park or around a city block. During the walk, celebrate in prayer the future benefits of the differences you bring to the relationship. (Repeat this walk weekly or until you begin to feel that the differences you bring to your marriage are truly celebrated!)

CHAPTER 3

Listening Your Way to Love

*Research has shown that 90 percent of our
struggles in marriage would be resolved if we
did nothing more than see that problem
from our partner's perspective.*
—Les and Leslie Parrot

A sk any group of people—friends, coworkers—"When do you feel loved?" and the answer will likely include something about listening. When people listen, we feel worthwhile—we feel valued. Listening is hard when trying to start a love relationship, because we'd rather try to impress. Yet listening is one of the strongest ways to say, "I love you."

Jesus's example in this startles us. Why the God-man with all the answers would wait to hear our questions is provocative. But that's just what Jesus did with the woman at the well. Though He knows immediately the answer to her need, He asks a question, listens, and waits for her response (see John 4). Why? Perhaps it is because, in knowing all things, He understands that His listening heart will be partly responsible for her healing.

A popular story tells of a little girl and a single mom who enter a toy store to buy a doll. As the little girl moves down the aisle, she asks her mother what each of the dolls can do. Some of the more expensive dolls walk, others talk, some sing or eat.

Finally, the little girl picks up a doll the young mother can afford. But, when the little girl asks what the doll can do, the mother notices there is no description on the box. Then an idea comes to her. She whispers to her daughter, "Honey, this doll listens."

Although the little girl knew nothing about the costs of the other dolls, she chose the one that listened. This quaint story speaks to the child who lives in each of us. Why? Because, when we can, we still choose people who listen.

An E.A.R. for Marriage

In the middle of every loving
heart is a listening E.A.R.

Most of us have seen "lonely people" on talk shows, in the malls, and in the cubicles where we work. Out of sight and out of touch, these individuals long for someone who can hear their hearts. Like the girl in the doll aisle, they are waiting for a box that reads, "This one listens." They want a marriage partner who is, to borrow the common expression, "all ears." Every marriage can benefit from improved listening skills. The following acrostic can help us remember that in the middle of every loving heart is a listening *ear*.

E—Enter their worlds

In his book *Caring Enough to Hear and Be Heard*, David Augsburger explains that, for effective listening to take place, we need to learn how to enter another person's world.[1] Entering

---

1. David Augsburger, *Caring Enough to Hear and Be Heard* (Ventura, CA: Regal Books, 1982), 38.

our partner's world will remove some of the communication barriers and help create an atmosphere where love can breathe. Sometimes entering our spouse's world means building bridges by attending an event with them, reading a book together, or asking open-ended questions. When our spouse knows that her world is becoming more important to us, she feels our love more deeply. When we work through conflict this is especially important. Understanding our partner's perspective can make it easier to find bridges we can cross together on the journey toward reconciliation.

A—Attend to the meaning behind their words

"You didn't listen to a thing I said!"

How many times do words like these crush a conversation? It's like we're giving an important recital of our thoughts and no one is in attendance. It's important to attend our partner's conversations. It's important to be there. When we aren't attending to the meaning behind our spouse's words, the conversation can seem like a kind of verbal air hockey—our words fly back and forth but seldom touch even the surface of our thoughts and feelings.

Solomon demonstrates this wisdom when he attends to the meaning behind his young bride's words: "Tell me, you whom I love, where you graze your flock and where you rest your sheep at midday. Why should I be like a veiled woman beside the flocks of your friends?" (Song of Songs 1:7). She seems to reprimand Solomon for making her chase after him like an immoral ("veiled") woman, because he failed to let her know where he was at "midday." The chorus, the "friends," answer her question "where?" by providing directions—"by the tents of the shepherds." Their response might represent the typical husband who responds to words instead of meanings. Earlier, she advises, "Do not stare at me because I am dark, because I am darkened by the sun . . . my own vineyard [her body] I have neglected" (Song of Songs 1:6). Solomon remembers her words. His wisdom recognizes that a woman's feelings about herself sometimes fashion her sentences. To love her, he compliments her beauty (v. 9) and makes a commitment to take time out of his schedule to make her "earrings of gold, studded with silver" (v. 11). He responds to her reprimand, not by defending himself or simply answering her question, but by attending to the meaning behind her words.

My wife, Linda, and I (Marty) have learned that our meanings are different. When I say, "I'm okay," I mean it's a good day. When she says, "I'm okay," it means she wants to talk about something that's troubling her. "Okay" can mean different things. It's important to discover the meanings behind our spouse's words.

R—Respond according to their needs

A youth director once told his youth group about the first time he kissed his fiancée. They were sitting beside a quiet stream when he asked, "Honey, can I kiss you?" She was silent. Although he considered the possibility that she didn't want to be kissed, he chose to believe she didn't hear him and asked again, "Can I kiss you?" She didn't respond. Frustrated and wondering if he had already ruined his opportunity, he persisted, increasing his volume, "Honey, can I kiss you?"

She was silent.

"Are you deaf?" he pleaded.

"Are you paralyzed?" she laughed.

The point is she wanted him to *respond*, appropriately, to the situation.

[***]

After we've *entered* our spouse's world and paid *attention* to the meaning behind his or her words, we can *respond* in a way that communicates, "I love you."

To encourage healthy conversation in the church, Paul wrote that we should build others up "according to their needs" (Ephesians 4:29). Entering each other's worlds helps us discover the other's "needs." Although Paul is specifically focusing on relationships within the body of Christ, his principle is especially relevant to marriage. In a romantic sense, when we fail to travel beyond our own worlds, we fail to understand and meet our spouse's needs, and we trade away the stars.

This is the model Jesus used when he *entered* our world, *attended* to the meaning behind our words, and *responded* in a breathtaking way to our needs. When we become all EARs, we can effectively love in a way our partner can hear. Every marriage can become more meaningful when we learn to listen our way to love.

Love Lock: Wife and Husband Appreciation Days

- Using your calendar, schedule a Wife or Husband Appreciation Day.

- Choose something you know your spouse likes (coffee, plants, a specific gift card) or a project your spouse needs help with (remodel, craft, designated chore) and acquire that something or complete that project.

- Place a note about the item you acquired or a note about the project you completed in an unusual location your spouse visits regularly (cabinet, silverware drawer, dryer).

- In the note, write something like "Happy Husband/ Wife Appreciation Day." When your spouse asks you what you're doing, say something like, "I'm starting a new tradition to say I love you."

(Note: This has been a favorite activity for many of our couples, so do this as often as it brings you joy!)

I Need to Feel Valued

Valued marriages begin with the determination to, first, become the unexpected friend.

CHAPTER 4

The Magic in a Kiss

Now a soft kiss—Aye, by that kiss,
I vow an endless bliss.
—John Keats

Traveling home from the premier of *Captain America*, our usually quiet, chick-flick-enthusiast daughter-in-law actually had something to say about the film. "Here's the question of the day," she began. "Would Captain America have defeated the Red Skull without Peggy's kiss?"

"Nope," my oldest, her husband, injected.

"Everything's about the kiss to you guys," my youngest teased. As we drove along discussing those things we agreed on—the well-blended attributes of the hero, the impressive CGI, the literary and historical allusions, and the testosterone-enhanced fight scenes, Allison's question replayed itself. There was something right, something insightful in her observation.

One of the lessons in Solomon's love story, the Song of Songs, is that there is inspiration in a kiss. In chapter four the husband announces, "Your lips drop sweetness as the honeycomb, my bride; milk and honey are under your tongue" (v. 11). Now that's a kiss! And since Solomon was writing around 900 BC, it's a kiss the French should not have received credit for. So why is writing about a kiss important to God?

The "milk and honey" combination wasn't introduced to the biblical text by Solomon. God had already described the Promised Land using the same phrase. Certainly such a description reminded Solomon's first readers and listeners of the amazing blessing of that land gift. By extension, those early readers understood that marriage's intimacy, with all of its milk-and-honey kisses, is a blessed gift too. But the combination of "milk and honey" is more than an allusion to the Promised Land; the contributions these foods make to the human diet are certainly the same for us as they were for the first readers of the Song of Songs.

The pleasures in all things sweet hasn't eluded the honey industry. According to the American Beekeeping Federation[1] and the *Statistical Abstracts of the United States,* honey production continues to rise and increase its economic value.[2] We like sweetness. We seem created for those honey-dipped pleasures (in appropriate amounts, of course, Proverbs 25:16).[3] The proteins and minerals in milk help us too. From infancy through old age, their properties minister to our bodies (and in that sense, to our whole person). So the comparison is an obvious one: milk-and-honey kisses provide more than erotic feelings. Put together, they represent how the right kiss can empower a man to be more the man he's meant to be. There is strength in passion's tender touch—a strength that our culture seldom discusses, a strength that my daughter-in-law rightly saw in Peggy and Captain America's kiss.

---

1. American Beekeeping Federation, www.abfnet.org, accessed August 1, 2011.

2 .US Census Bureau, *Statistical Abstract of the United States*: 201; Table 860, 551.

3. J. F. Walvoord, R. B. Zuck, and Dallas Theological Seminary, *The Bible Knowledge Commentary: An Exposition of the Scriptures* (Wheaton, IL: Victor Books, 1989), SoS 4:11.

Whether or not the kiss did inspire the mythical hero remains for the audience to decide; however, there can be no myth in our understanding of the power of intimate expressions between couples who want to live beyond themselves. Solomon's bride (probably Lady Wisdom) echoes this truth in the first chapter of the Song of Songs, when she, aroused by his mythical character, sings, "Let him kiss me with the kisses of his mouth. . . . Your name is like perfume poured out" (vv. 2–3). Before Solomon (probably Wisdom personified) gave himself over to the sins he mentioned in Ecclesiastes, his character (his "name") was extravagant. That rare "perfume poured out" kind of character, caused Solomon's bride to long for his kisses.

What made this husband's character so kissable? Part of the answer is found in the way he sacrificed his time and energy to love her out loud. In trying to help her with her low opinion of herself at the beginning of their marriage, Solomon complimented her beauty *in front* of her friends and involved others in the making of a gift for her. "I liken you my darling to a mare harnessed to one of the chariots of Pharaoh. . . . We will make you earrings of gold, studded with silver" (Song of Songs 1:9, 11).

This kind of outward demonstration of his affection required a sacrifice of time and effort. It is part of what changed her feelings about herself. It's the Bible's wisdom, showing us once again, that loving someone out loud can change that person's self-perceptions, as well as the way they perceive the one doing the loving. Loving out loud makes a person's character kissable.

Although Cap only lives in the minds of those who want to spend a few movie moments in a world where courage and unselfishness ink heroes into our hearts, the inspiration in a real kiss, a kiss infused with character, follows us long after the credits roll.

In sixty years of combined ministry to couples, Rich and I have learned that intimacy promotes more than children and a temporary satisfaction of delightful urges. We have seen many lives changed by married love. We've observed, too, as my oldest son likes to express, that although we often want others to see the "director's cut" of our marriage story, God and the people who really know us see the unrated, uncut version. The truth is, all of us can tell the difference between a kiss that inspires a man to love heroically and a kiss that keeps him in his own little world. With that said, maybe one scene in a movie like *Captain America* can help us see God's purposes more clearly. Maybe the kiss between two people who have sacrificed their lives for others can inspire our understanding of an ancient biblical text with not-so-ancient applications.

Love Lock: Loving Out Loud

- Using your calendar, schedule a day where you can visit where your husband or wife works or a place your spouse likes to hang out with friends (a team, hobby group, or Bible study, etc.)

- Purchase a card, a balloon, and flowers (or a couple of favorite snacks).

- Take these items to the place and set them in the lunchroom or another prominent location. (Check ahead to get permission to do this.)

- In a text or phone message, say something like "I love to love you out loud, because you are a person whose character excites me! I left a surprise in your lunchroom today (or other place where you left the items)."

(Note: This kind of love makes you kissable! Have fun with that.)

CHAPTER 5

Editing Expectations

*When you stop expecting people to be perfect,
you can like them for who they are.*
—Donald Miller

It stunned the critics. Despite being dubbed a low-budget, small-town documentary, *October Sky,* a movie based on the life of NASA engineer Homer Hickam, rocketed up the charts. Apparently, the story of four friends fighting the community expectations that tried to bury their dreams in the coal mines of West Virginia orbited close to home. But these were not the only expectations viewers identified with.

Throughout the movie, Homer struggles with the expectations of a father who wants him to follow in his footsteps. When his dad finally relents and tells Homer he can follow in the career path of his "rocket science hero, Dr. Von Braun," Homer replies, "Dr. Von Braun's a great scientist, but he isn't my hero."

This powerful declaration from a son who appreciated his father, despite the agonizing expectations he placed on him, resonated with audiences. Why? Because Homer somehow found the strength to survive the burden most of us bear at one time or another—the burden of expectations.

Expectations can either make couples feel worlds apart or closer together. Editing expectations involves understanding why we have the expectations we have, and understanding why we have them means understanding each other in a deeper way. My wife might have an expectation that comes from a childhood wound. Once I understand that, I understand her better, and the reason behind her expectation now affords me the luxury of valuing her in a way I didn't know she needed. That's the power of editing our expectations. But, it isn't that easy.

Each of us has expectations that help us formulate and identify satisfaction in our relationships. Bosses have lists for employees; employees have lists for their bosses; friends carry lists for each other, as do husbands for wives and wives for husbands. Expectations come from experiences, friends, value systems, families, cultures, churches, the Bible, and our entertainment choices. Every relationship is in some way governed by expectations. Some expectations benefit us and cause growth. Others, especially unrealistic and hidden expectations, bury our dreams.

The following list shows how expectations impact our marriages and why it's important for us to learn how to edit.

Unmet Expectations Intensify Minor Issues

If putting the cap on the toothpaste is important to us, then each day we find the tube without the lid fastened, the expectation moves closer to being of primary importance—even though, logically, it isn't. This is why minor issues often become major irritants. When the expectation reaches the top of our list of unmet expectations, divorce is a toothbrush away!

Expectations Put Us in a Parental Role

Whenever our spouse doesn't comply with our list of expectations, we find ourselves using parental language, "If you had done _____, this would never have happened." This makes our partner feel like a teenager again (and those are years many of us don't want to relive).

Expectations Reduce the Relationship to a Performance

"For better or for worse . . ." Most couples mean these vows—until the "worse" part includes living with unmet expectations. When this happens, we stop ice dancing to the careful choreography our spouse created. We slip and slide our way through the routine, but we don't measure up. The relationship becomes a performance, not the combination of planned and spontaneous elements God wanted us to cut up the ice with. We begin to feel loved only for saying and doing the right things—not for being the right person. Paul reminded us in Romans 5:8 that "while we were still sinners, Christ died for us." We need to remind ourselves that our love should never be based on how our spouse performs. It needs to be based on who she or he is before God.

Expectations Create High-Maintenance Relationships

It is almost impossible to feel valued in a High maintenance relationship. These relationships require constant attention and energy to attain what should feel relaxed and natural. I (Marty) could have asked my wife, Linda, to write this section. Most of our early conflicts resulted from my unrealistic expectations.

One Saturday morning I "invited" Linda to help me replace the clutch in our Datsun B210. After jacking up the car and setting it on stands, I rested the transmission on my brand-new hydraulic floor jack and slid under the car. As I loosened the last bolt from the housing, I asked Linda to lower the floor jack so that I could carefully slide the transmission out of the way. The next thing I knew, the housing was in the middle of my chest! I yelled, "Raise the jack!" Linda began pumping the handle frantically. The transmission didn't budge. The only thing that moved was hydraulic fluid squirting out the jack's valve each time she pumped the handle. Thinking that I was dying under the car, she broke into tears.

Although she laughs about it now, I should never have put her in that situation. She'd never worked on a car. She'd never used a floor jack. The emotional conflict I created came from my unrealistic expectations. And trust me, it wasn't the last maintenance we had to do in our marriage!

Share Your List

Redeeming a marriage damaged by expectations involves understanding the differences between hidden and unrealistic expectations. Many counselors believe that most relational conflict caused by expectations disappears when hidden expectations are brought out into the open. Reviewing your list will help you reduce the frequency of conflicts caused by expectations and help your partner "feel" valued.

Hand Over the List

1. Sit down together and write out on a napkin or a 3×5 card one expectation each of you "feels" is unrealistic.

2. Share your unrealistic expectation without discussing any solutions.

3. Spend time in separate prayer, then meet again to discuss how the unrealistic expectation makes you "feel."

4. Check to see if the "unrealistic" expectation reflects anything the Bible says is important. If it is a clear expectation from God, it's not unrealistic. However, if you have to spin

Scripture to make it fit some expectation you'd like to have fulfilled in your marriage, that's dishonest. Focus on God's grace toward us, His patient love, His mercy, His sacrificial character. You should be able to agree that if the expectation isn't found anywhere in the Bible, it is unrealistic.

Handing over the list will allow you to be honest about the unrealistic expectations you put on your spouse. This honesty will help the one you love feel valued.

Admit Areas of Immaturity

1. Choose one expectation that, although you admit it is "unrealistic," you feel too immature to handle without help. (Your conversation should sound like this: "I can't handle you leaving the lid off the toothpaste. I know it's unrealistic. I'm working on it and praying about it, but right now, I just need you to help me with it.")

2. Each week after church services, review the lists. This will help you value each other at a deeper level, and it will help you practice Paul's instruction to "put off falsehood and speak truthfully to his neighbor" (Ephesians 4:25).

Impossible Expectations

Let's not pretend editing expectations is always easy. For example, expectations are difficult to change when they come from perfectionists—people who are perfect at arguing, at manipulating, at everything except editing their expectations. A perfectionist's fear of being found out (yes, most of them realize they aren't perfect) short-circuits their kindness. All their anxiety and angst is directed at their closest friend (the person they feel most relaxed around)—which, if you haven't guessed already, just happens to be you.

So what can we do? Since some conflicts caused by unrealistic expectations won't diminish by handing over the list or admitting areas of immaturity, the best place to start is to take our focus off our own pain. Although this may appear counterproductive, focusing on our spouse's pain will change the frequency of conflicts created by his or her unrealistic expectations. If you can learn to see the pain beyond yours, you won't immediately feel valued in the relationship, but you will begin to understand your spouse in a deeper way. Eventually, this new understanding will help you feel more significant.

Mr. Hickam showed his son he valued him, when he let go of his expectations. Instead of burying Homer's dreams with his own in the coal mines of West Virginia, he encouraged Homer to reach for the moon—which is exactly where Homer's efforts in NASA landed mankind two decades later.

Our resolutions may not orbit the silver screen in a movie like *October Sky*, but they will help our spouses feel valued and honor all of heaven. And maybe, just maybe, our willingness to understand the expectations of the person we've chosen to love will create in us the character of a hero.

Love Lock: Editing Expectations

- Choose a movie you've already seen or a book you've read together recently.

- As you re-watch or re-read, look for the first evidence of a character who is burdened by an expectation. Then, pause the movie or your reading of the book.

- Pretend, together, that you are rewriting the script and deleting the expectation from this scene. What would happen to the story's ending if you left the expectation out?

- Discuss how God might be using one expectation you face from others (or from each other, if you're brave). How might He be using the expectation to compose your love story?

CHAPTER 6

Shelving Expectations

When I (Rich) was in seminary, I also worked full-time at a local hospital and spoke at various churches on the weekends. LouAnna was home each day with our newborn and a two-year-old. She saw our Saturdays as opportunities to become reacquainted and make improvements on our love nest. I longed for time to study and sleep.

We each had a hidden list of expectations and valued each other less when our expectations were not met. The "shelves incident" drew our attention to the problem.

One Saturday morning we were standing in our garage, surveying the mess that had slowly backed our cars onto the driveway. We looked across the street at our neighbor's garage. I noticed their nice cars. LouAnna noticed their nice garage.

"Look at the shelves they have!"

I acknowledged that they had shelves, stumbled back into the house and subtracted "clean the garage" from my Saturday "to-do" list. While I subtracted, LouAnna added. That morning her list looked like this:

1. Spends time with me and the kids
2. Stays on his diet
. . . .

25. Builds shelves

Two weeks later, we visited the local hardware store. For some reason we stopped in front of the shelving display. Again, LouAnna mentioned "how nice it would be to have shelves in our garage." I thought that working full-time, attending seminary, and ministering on the weekends were "nice" things too. I thought they demonstrated the tremendous value I placed on our relationship. Shelves were not on any list that I knew about. At this point, her list looked like this:

1. Spends time with me and the kids
2. Stays on his diet
. . . .
5. Builds shelves

In two weeks the shelves had moved from #25 to #5!

Several more weeks went by, and we found ourselves again standing on an even smaller patch of garage floor. LouAnna said, "When are you going to get those shelves?"

"Shelves?"

I sensed tension. The list now read,

1. Builds shelves
2. Builds shelves now!
3. Spends time with me and the kids
4. Stays on his diet

You should see the shelves in our garage!

Excuse the pun, but in marriage, it's important to learn to "shelve" our expectations, to replace them with a deeper understanding of the kinds of things that make our spouse feel important. In our counseling, Marty and I often use Paul's words to help young couples work through expectations. The Apostle

Paul told the church at Philippi, "Each of you should look not only to your own interests, but also to the interests of others" (Philippians 2:4).

The principle of looking to each other's interests can help us avoid expecting our wives or husbands to meet our own. The following principles can help us learn to shelve our expectations.

Each unrealistic expectation is like a link
in a heavy chain that increasingly
binds us to a disappointing marriage.
—Les and Leslie Parrott

Step 1: Hand Over the List

Sit down, list your expectations, and hand them to your spouse. Family therapist Paul Coleman suggests that rehearsing specific phrases can help us convey our concerns in a tender and honest manner.[1] When handing over the list, the conversation could go something like, "I value you and want to improve our relationship. I believe that we may be in conflict over what we expect from each other. Let's pray that our lists will promote empathy."

Step 2: Prioritize the List

The "shelving incident" forced LouAnna and me to hand over our lists. We discovered that she was unaware of some of my expectations and I was unaware of hers. We prioritized our lists and decided we would focus on the important issues and work

---

1. Paul Coleman, *How to Say It for Couples: Communicating with Tenderness, Openness and Honesty* (New Jersey: Prentice Hall Press, 2002).

on the others later. Prioritizing is easier if we remember a few guidelines:

- First list, then define.
- Avoid emotional statements. "Would you please pick up your clothes?" is better than "Our room is a pigsty!" The second statement could push our spouses toward resentment and bitterness.
- Move character qualities such as kindness to the top of the list. Unfortunately, we often trade these character qualities for things like clean rooms.

Step 3: Compare the Lists to Scripture

In our premarital discipleship, Linda and I (Marty) have the couples use a Bible site or concordance to search for key words in their lists and ask the following:

- "Does the Bible put the item in the same place on the list I do?"
- "Will my list help grow the fruit of the Spirit in my life? (see Galatians 5:22)

If the answer to any of these is "no," you'll need to change your list so that the items line up with what God says will add value to your relationship. Often it is wise to seek the advice of an older, happily married couple in your church. They can help you list the most important items first. For example, items like, "pick up your stuff," should be placed after items like, "when under duress, speak to each other with kindness." "Picking up stuff" is a task; "kindness" is a character quality (Ephesians 4:32) and fruit of the Spirit (Galatians 5:22).

Before you have a misunderstanding,
get an understanding.
—Richard Davis

Step 4: Lock the Lists

Keep the list between you, your spouse, and your mentoring couple. Avoid using the lists to respond to recent frictions or frustrations. Limit the number of items. Too many items confuse the conversation.

Step 5: Pray Through the Lists

James wrote that in the middle of trials we can pray for wisdom and God will give it abundantly (James 1:5). Before you pray, reaffirm your belief that having shared expectations will enhance the relationship. Pray in a neutral place where you can sit for an extended period.

Step 6: Empathize the List

Start with observations and questions. "I found it interesting that you included _____ on your list. Why is this important to you? Why is this important to us?"

Beginning this way allows the meeting to start without confrontation. Focus your energies on understanding what your spouse is saying, rather than on trying to get him or her to understand you. Don't try to "sell" or "spin" your list.

Step 7: Draw the Line

The line is the barrier that discourages expectations below it from moving up the list. Everything above the line formulates the important issues you agree to work on. (See chapter 5, "Editing

Expectations.") At this point, agree that items below the line should not affect how valued you feel. Remember, you should show patience and deference, but you cannot let someone's list govern your life. You must draw the line.

Step 8: Periodically Review the List

The day after a birthday or Thanksgiving or New Year's is a good time to review your lists. (You'll begin to associate that day with the good things that come from this exercise.)

Something as simple as a hidden expectation can ruin a relationship, but something as simple as writing a list together can redeem it. We hope these time-tested steps can help each of us feel more deeply valued by the one we love. We hope, too, that learning to value each other in this way will help us assemble the right pieces and turn even our "shelving incidents" into, well, nice garages.

Love Lock: Shelving Expectations

- Use a Bible site or concordance to help you study one expectation from the list you made in Step 3 above. Use synonyms if you can't find your word.

- Then ask the following questions about the word you chose:

  - Does the Bible put the item in the same place on the list I do?"
  - "Will my list help grow the fruit of the Spirit in my life? (see Galatians 5:22)

- If the answer to any of these is "no," you'll need to shelve it so that your expectations line up with what God says will add value to your relationship.

- If the Bible indicates that the expectation will grow the fruit of the Spirit in your lives, we suggest meeting with church staff or an older and wiser couple. They can give you ideas about how to add the fruit of the Spirit.

CHAPTER 7

Tracking Storms

Resolving disagreements can also "un-stick"
a couple, moving the two of you to new
levels of intimacy and growth. Some of the
closest moments a couple can experience
often arrive after resolving conflicts.
—Mitch Temple

Alex and Megan had been dating for several months and had discussed the possibility of getting married. Alex was one of those overly confident guys. He seemed to enjoy making people uncomfortable with how much he knew. Megan wondered if he ever thought about how his "knowledge" affected his friendships. The one-upmanship made Megan feel less valued. Their time together was enjoyable as long as Megan didn't hit Alex's "I'm a superior person" button. Once that button was tapped, Megan knew she could forget any encouraging or meaningful conversation.

Alex created a climate in their relationship that was like the eye of a tropical storm, peaceful for a period with disaster lurking at the edges. Such uneasiness creates a tension that makes it difficult to relax, because we never know when the wreckage will start flying around our heads. Some of her church friends had noticed the storm warnings. A few had tried to tell her that most relationships don't survive such tempests. Megan ignored their concerns—she kept trying to convince them (and herself) that she "loved Alex." Megan learned the hard way that "real love" notices when the climate changes—that "discerning love" tracks the storms (Philippians 1:9).

> *The way we communicate with others*
> *and with ourselves ultimately determines*
> *the quality of our lives.* —Anthony Robbins

Storm Warnings

The climates we create affect the amount of pleasure we receive from marriage. I (Rich) learned the concept of creating the right climate from Dr. John Lange. Asked to teach leadership to a class of officers in the military, John was determined to help them discover the importance of climate. As the class progressed, the students discovered that Dr. Lange was a caring instructor—he promised he'd never give a pop quiz and even brought donuts to class. However, the evening he was teaching about the importance of communication climate, there were no donuts. A commander entered the room, smiled at Lange and cleared his throat.

"I want to ask about last week's assignment."

"Commander, last week's assignment was written at the eighth-grade reading level. If you need clarification, you don't belong in this class." Lange was determined to let his students "experience the lesson." The Commander, embarrassed, muttered some obscenities and made his way back to his chair.

Next, Dr. Lange indicated that he was going to give a test on the reading material—a test which would comprise 50 percent of their grade. Some tried to remind him that he said he wouldn't do this, but he merely replied that he was in charge. When Lange stated that "time was up," a colonel was still writing. Lange walked over to him, yanked his paper from the desk, walked to the garbage can and dropped it in.

"Colonel, when I say time is up, it is up. You have failed the test."

Then Lange slowly moved to the board and wrote:

YOUR LEADERSHIP STYLE
CREATES A CLIMATE.

It took the class several minutes to realize they had just experienced the lesson. Lange had created a harsh, inflexible, and confusing climate on purpose. We might assume it was an important lesson for those military personnel, but the truth is, it's a lesson for all of us.

The negative climate Dr. Lange created on purpose, most of us create by accident. Communication climates forecast how valued we will feel in a relationship.

Measure the Precipitation

Linda and I (Marty) ask the couples we counsel the following question: "What kind of climate do you create in your marriage?" Their answers help us help them address not only the quality of their relationship, but the details that encourage or discourage closeness.

Jesus created a climate that drew people to him. His humility and gentleness fill the stories of the New Testament with a kind of experience that interprets "holiness" for the reader. Born in a manger, he lived with "no place to lay his head" (Luke 9:58) and died on the worst instrument of punishment human beings had created. His life communicated humility.

Paul told the church at Ephesus to follow Jesus Christ's example. "Be completely humble and gentle; be patient, bearing with one another in love" (Ephesians 4:2).

Humility and gentleness are key measures in marriage. They help us instill value and they help us create communication climates that warm hearts and invigorate spirits—climates that attract our spouses to the person of Christ inside us.

The climate Alex created in his relationship with Megan wasn't "gentle." Instead it blew like a harsh wind through Megan's view of her value as a human being. And there certainly wasn't much "humility," as his one-upmanship continued to embarrass her in front of her family and friends.

Alex had never thought about what it might take to create a communication climate that made Megan feel the same way God felt about her. Alex was not only ignorant about how the communication climate he had created affected their relationship, he also really didn't care.

Megan kept hoping that good weather was just around the corner. She looked and longed so desperately for change that she saw change when there was none. Eventually, they both began waking up early each morning, fearing the icy chill carried on the winds of every condescending conversation.

Rich and I have met with many Megans years after they've married. Within the first painful minutes, we often hear sentiments like, "People tried to tell me, but I didn't listen. I fell in love and the rest is history." If they'd only understood that the communication climate often determines whether that "history" reads like a World War documentary or a romantic biography.

Speak when you are angry - and you'll make the best speech you'll ever regret. —Laurence J. Peter

Hoping that "humility" and "gentleness" will eventually show up isn't enough. When the climate in a relationship turns cold and the storms begin, we have to start measuring the precipitation. Once we begin "measuring," we can begin walking out from under the clouds.

Connecting

Before we married, we decided to get individual counseling—in addition to the two-hour marriage counseling session. We didn't feel we were able to be honest about sensitive, possibly controversial topics, especially in front of the person we knew we wanted to keep at all costs. We knew it took an unusually mature person to be able to think critically about the decision to marry, so we sought out individual counselors. We suggest it to every couple we meet! —Liz and David (married 27 years)

Tracking the Storms: A Communication Activity for Couples

Tracking the times and situations in which couples hurt each other can improve the communication climate. At first this kind of activity sounds counterproductive, the opposite of forgiveness. However, this counseling tool involves documenting when you know you've hurt your spouse rather than when you've been hurt by critical or condescending words. That's the difference.

It's so easy to fall into the routine of recording the other's wounds, but that kind of record-keeping increases the storm's momentum. By contrast, writing or typing into a calendar when we've hurt the one we love helps us become more honest and "humble" about our part in the relational storms.

After a week or two of this exercise, you can (and should) erase the evidence. (Throw the calendar away or delete its content). The point of the activity is that it helps to see the storms on paper, to track them. This simple exercise promotes our understanding of not only how often we contribute to the storms but also of the kinds of words and actions that stir them.

Communication works for those who work at it.
—John Powell

Tracking the kinds of words and actions that devalue our spouses helps us become aware of the pain they cause and the turmoil they create. We end up staring at a piece of paper that reminds us there are words we can avoid and behaviors we can change.

The "humility" required for this kind of exercise creates a stronger kind of "gentleness" in our spirits. Where we might have grown indignant or distant, the humility in writing down our own failures encourages forgiveness and closeness. We find understanding growing in our hearts. The understanding melts our bitterness and warms up a new kind of "patience" in our attitude. Our spouse begins to sense the change in temperature, the warm breeze and sunshine.

Unlike the fixed weather systems God created, our relationships are governed by the climates we create. Paul's counsel can help us transform the relational storms, like Alex and Megan experienced, into communication climates where calm and contentment shine through the character traits of humility and gentleness. Where both individuals feel valued and appreciated for the gifts they bring. That's what tracking storms can do.

Love Lock: Sharing the Comforter

- Create a three-column chart on a napkin or any piece of paper.

- Title the first column "Words that Help me Feel Appreciated," then list the words (or phrases) in that column. Try to limit yourself to six words.

- Title the second column, "Actions that Help me Feel Appreciated," then list the actions in that column. Try to limit yourself to three actions.

- Title the third column, "Scriptures that Help me Feel Appreciated," then list Scriptures in that column. Use your phone or a concordance to look for examples.

- Now get under a comforter together and share your lists.

This simple activity will help you get to know how to communicate with each other. The closeness it can create will warm your relationship and help you weather the storms!

I Need to Feel a Part of You

All married couples should learn the art of battle as they should learn the art of making love. Good battle is objective and honest—never vicious or cruel. Good battle is healthy and constructive, and brings to a marriage the principles of equal partnership.
—Anne Landers

CHAPTER 8

Promoting Partnership

In my mind, marriage is a spiritual partnership and
union in which we willingly give and receive love,
create and share intimacy, and open ourselves to be
available and accessible to another human being in
order to heal, learn and grow. —Iyania Vanzant

When Dan became a "partner" at his law firm, several families at our church celebrated his new position. Though our knowledge about Dan's promotion was gleaned mostly from *Perry Mason* and *Law & Order,* we knew that it meant an increase in respect and the realization that he was now a more prominent part of the team. God uses a similar comparison to help couples feel more a part of each other.

Husbands, in the same way be considerate
as you live with your wives, and treat them
with respect as the weaker partner and as
heirs with you of the gracious gift of life,
so that nothing will hinder your prayers.
1 Peter 3:7

The apostle Peter's words must have startled his generation. Marriage certainly wasn't a partnership when Peter was writing. Unfortunately, Rich and I have seen too many marriages patterned after Peter's culture, where husbands and wives live, as songwriter Bob Bennett put it, "together all alone."

The Jury's Out

It seems ironic that some husbands, rather than focusing on phrases like "be considerate" and "treat them with respect," read too much into the term "weaker." The New International Version translators wisely inserted the word *partner* to receive the Greek adjective "weaker" so that it would clarify the concept of the rest of the sentence—that wives are "heirs with you of the gracious gift of life."

When two people marry, they form a partnership as "heirs" together of the "gift of life." Although this is a gift from heaven, the state also recognizes the equality of that arrangement. We have interviewed hundreds of couples who miss so much of the "gift" because they have never related to each other as partners. Partners do things together. They decide things together. They have deference for each other and are hesitant to make decisions without the other person having input. In a law firm, partnerships build mutual respect, increase motivation and strengthen trust. Although these are also important in marriage, marriage's partnership prospers most when it shares equality, leadership, and decision-making.

Equality

*It is often the struggle for superiority that
creates inequality in our relationships.*

If you think about your best friends, you'll notice one common characteristic that defines your relationship—equality. If we feel superior or inferior to a person, we struggle to establish a friendship. Friendships require equality. Partnerships require the same thing. In *Women, Men, and the Trinity*, Dr. Nancy Hedberg explains that it is often the struggle for superiority that creates inequality in our relationships.[1]

Lois and Fred struggled with inequality. Fred was a multi-talented pastor who led his young marriage by dictum and command. He would deny that he was an autocrat, but everyone around him knew the truth. Fred wasn't a team player. He worked well with an Elders board as long as they followed his instructions. He considered them a "sounding board" rather than fellow leaders. Like many husbands who are in leadership positions outside the home, he carried that same superiority into his marriage.

Even though Lois worked full-time, she always had dinner ready for him—he liked it that way. One night, when he entered the kitchen, things were different. He saw a note lying on the empty table.

> *"I'm done, I can't take it anymore. I don't want to hurt or embarrass you, but I can't keep living this way. I am tired of being your slave. I thought that after we were married, your attitude would improve. I was wrong."*

Fred's first thought was, "What will I tell the church?" Instead of being hurt or ashamed at the possibility of losing his wife, he became angry because this would embarrass him. Fred had to resign his ministry. He and Lois are still separated, but after

---

1. Nancy Hedberg. *Women, Men, and the Trinity* (Eugene, OR: Wipf and Stock Publishers, 2010).

months of counseling, they are beginning to discover the meaning of a partnership they never had.

Fred is learning that people don't experience friendship unless they are treated with equality. Prior to the counseling, it had never occurred to him that his wife was also supposed to be a leader. Paul said it this way in reference to young widows: "So I counsel younger widows to marry, to have children, to manage their homes and to give the enemy no opportunity for slander" (1 Timothy 5:14).

The phrase "manage their homes" is the translation of a single Greek word which literally means "despot of the house." Although Paul writes to the church in Ephesus that the husband is the head of the wife (signifying the nurturing relationship Christ has with the church), wives are told to "manage their homes." When you combine what Peter and Paul wrote, the wife is a partner, a fellow believer, and the manager of the home. That's the equality God describes.

Spiritual Leadership

When Marty and I ask groups of Christian couples to identify the most important quality a Christian husband should exhibit in the home, over 90 percent respond with something related to "spiritual leadership." If you ask the same groups about the most important quality a wife should possess, the answers are divided between words like "helpful" and "loving." Most couples are surprised when we suggest that "spiritual leadership" is the biblical norm for both men and women. The Bible teaches every believer to be spiritually controlled. Notice what Paul said to the church at Ephesus.

Do not get drunk on wine, which leads to debauchery. Instead, be filled with the Spirit. Speak to one another with psalms, hymns and spiritual

songs. Sing and make music in your heart to the
Lord, always giving thanks to God the Father for
everything, in the name of our Lord Jesus Christ.
Submit to one another out of reverence for Christ.
Ephesians 5:18–21

In the original, this passage is one sentence. The main verb, "be filled," implies control in a similar way that wine controls. When we are controlled by the Holy Spirit, the way we speak to one another is filled with spiritually mature influence. We have a heart filled with song, and we are constantly giving thanks for all things (good and bad) in our lives. The Bible teaches that whether serving as "head" or "manager" of the home, every believer's leadership is to be spiritually controlled—continually creating the feeling that we belong together, that we are part of each other.

Connecting

From the beginning, we talked about the wisdom in working together to decide how we were going to handle finances, household duties, working outside the home, having children, disciplining and raising them, and other priorities. We're so glad we did!

We also found an older couple to mentor us. Our motto became, "When you need help, get help—but always together!"

—Wayne and Lynn (married 47 years)

Shared Decisions

It is interesting that Paul never referred to the husband as the head of the home. He said that he was the head of the wife. Much has been written about the roles of men and women in the home, and our goal is not to rehearse the debate. Scripture reminds us that though Eve sinned first, it is through Adam that sin entered the human race (Romans 5:12). Eve was deceived, but Adam made a conscious choice. Choosing between obedience to God and the possibility of losing Eve, he chose to keep Eve and lose God (Genesis 3). The point is that through the second Adam, Jesus Christ, husbands are accountable to God for their decisions—not that they are the only decision-makers in the home.

Dr. David Olson, the CEO of Prepare-Enrich (a relational assessment service) explains an additional value of shared leadership. His research, concentrated around the question "In your relationship is there a sharing of leadership and decisions?", suggests that couples who answer "no" enjoy less relational satisfaction.[2]

Failing to share leadership and decision-making was a large part of the reason Lois and Fred separated and pursued counseling. Treating Lois more like a doer than a thinker, defrauded their friendship and diminished her experiences as an intelligent woman. As a result, they seldom felt a part of each other.

Marriage's friendship deepens and means more when we promote each other to the position of "partner." Like our attorney friend, contented couples learn to celebrate the equality, shared spiritual leadership, and decision-making that promote connection and secure the kind of partnership we all long for.

---

2. David Olson, Amy Olson-Sigg, and Peter J. Larson, *The Couple Checkup* (Nashville: Thomas Nelson, 2008).

*Many persons have a wrong idea of what
constitutes true happiness. It is not
attained through self-gratification but through
fidelity to a worthy purpose.* —Helen Keller

Love Lock: Collaborating Couples

- Choose an art, remodeling, service, or other project that you could work on together.

- Design a date around discussing how to approach the project.

- At some convenient time during the date, draw a storyboard of the steps it will take to complete the project. (Note to artists: Don't worry about the quality of the pictures at this point.)

- Under each picture in the storyboard, write the name of the person who will oversee that part of the project. This promotes partnership.

- Chose a start date and begin following your storyboard together.

- Have fun!

CHAPTER 9

One + One = One?

O ne plus one never equaled one in our math classrooms, so why do we assume it will in our living rooms? The pronouncement from Mark 8:10 "the two will become one" sounds romantic at the wedding, but when the test comes, it feels like a thirteen-page story problem waiting to flunk us. Why is it so hard to learn the new math?

It's hard because we often start from the wrong suppositions. For instance, we're taught that marriage equals happiness. Though the statement's true in a way, we are uncomfortable with its inverse—that marriage is also a cause of conflict. The sooner we accept that fact, the sooner we'll be able to experience a deeper sense of being part of each other.

> *A happy home is one in which each spouse grants*
> *the possibility that the other might be right, though*
> *neither believes it.* —Dan Fraser

Story Problem

Think about the last conflict you had with your spouse or fiancé. Maybe as you "discussed" issues, pointed out options, and hammered at supporting materials, you finally decided it wasn't worth the effort (after all, there was a slight possibility you could be wrong). Although it's the wrong decision, it is common for couples to believe their marriage can survive using this kind of avoidance. However, the Scriptures show us that this kind of problem solving doesn't pencil out.

After making man, God explains that it isn't good for him to be alone (Genesis 2:18). So He creates Eve from Adam's own genetic material (his rib). The Hebrew poetry here implies that they complemented each other. We have no idea how much time elapses between chapters 2 and 3, but we do know that a problem is introduced into the story.

In chapter 3, the serpent tempts Eve. "God knows that when you eat of it [the Tree of the Knowledge of Good and Evil] your eyes will be opened, and you will be like God, knowing good and evil" (v. 5). Although it wasn't a lie (Afterward, in verse 22, God says, "The man has now become like one of us, knowing good and evil.") it introduces a sad irony: that in becoming like God we became separated from him and each other.

Later, after explaining the consequences of Adam's action, God turns his attention to Eve. "To the woman he [God] said, 'I will greatly increase your pains in childbearing; with pain you will give birth to children. Your desire will be for your husband, and he will rule over you' " (Genesis 3:16).

This is one of the most misunderstood passages of Scripture. The last sentence of verse 16 has traditionally been interpreted this way: "You will have sexual desire for your husband, and he will be in charge of you." However, as many Old Testament scholars have pointed out, the context is concerned with more than "sexual desire." The same Hebrew word that translates as "desire" occurs again in Genesis chapter 4.

> *Then the Lord said to Cain, "Why are you angry?*
> *Why is your face downcast? If you do what is right,*
> *will you not be accepted? But if you do not do what*

is right, sin is crouching at your door; it desires to
have you, but you must master it."
Genesis 4:6–7

The word is used in chapter 4 to imply control. What, then, was God saying to Eve in chapter 3? Ron Allen suggests the following:

> *I will also allow pain to come into your marriage*
> *relationship with your husband. You will tend to*
> *desire to usurp the role I have given to him as the*
> *compassionate leader in your home, rejecting his*
> *role and belittling his manhood. And the man on*
> *his part will tend to relate to you in loveless tyranny,*
> *dominating and stifling your integrity as an equal*
> *partner to himself.*[1]

From that day on, conflict divided the husband-wife relationship. With the death, burial, and resurrection of Jesus, the second Adam, we now have the means to change the equation. In Ephesians 5, Paul exhorts husbands to love their wives, indicating that marriage should reflect the love of Christ, not the discord in the Garden of Eden. But Paul also gives us God's solution to the conflict introduced in Eden. "Each one of you also must love his wife as he loves himself, and the wife must respect her husband" (Ephesians 5:33).

Because he created us, God knows that men need respect and women need love.

Dr. Emerson Eggerichs launched Love and Respect Conferences to explain this reality. He teaches that women need to be loved and tend to interpret their relationships based on that

---

1. Ron Allen. *The Majesty of Man: The Dignity of Being Human* (Portland: Multnomah Press, 1984), 147.

need. Therefore, men need to be respected and interpret their relationships based on that need.

Connecting

We write things we appreciate about each other on sticky notes throughout the year and drop them in our "Thanksgiving Box." During the holiday, we open the box and read the cards to each other.

Through the years we've noticed how little statements like, "I was sick and you washed the car" or "I loved watching you play with the children at church" have helped us grow in our respect for each other.

We date the notes, so that as we read them, we can stick them in chronological order into a photo album we call our "Book of Memories." We think it's part of the reason we've become best friends!

—Demetri and Elena (married 36 years)

Once they're shown respect, most men will feel loved. Contrary to their natural tendency, wives need to stop trying to control their husbands. A godly wife brings out the potential she sees in her husband by respecting him.

Respect is important because each of us was made in the image of God. When her husband is "acting like he's eighteen again," a wise wife knows when and how to remind him of his real age. She doesn't choose words that make him feel less a part of the relationship. She doesn't "put him down." She shows respect in her language and gestures.

In God's plan, the husband can't be either a dictator or a doormat. His privilege is to become the lover of his wife. Instead of commanding her, he cherishes her. Instead of bossing, he blesses her. Instead of giving in or taking control, he gently controls the give and take. He understands that his wife needs to feel loved, not just be loved.

Marriage isn't two people controlling each other; it's two people controlled by a deep love and respect for each other. Only when we understand God's solution for this kind of conflict in marriage, can we begin to solve the inherent problem in the marriage story. Then we'll discover the result of God's marital math: that one + one can = one.

Love Lock: Using the New Math

- Design a date around discussing how you might participate in each other's hobbies.

- At a convenient time during the date, take turns sharing what about your lover's presence would mean the most to you while you're participating in your hobby.

- Using your calendar, map out for one month when you will begin participating together.

- Sharing each other's hobbies can be a powerful way of increasing your experience of oneness.

CHAPTER 10

Defining Definitions

*What we believe in marriage determines what we
receive in marriage.*

Paul and Juanita had decided to divorce. Linda and I (Marty) had met with this couple for several months. From the first counseling session, I was amazed their marriage had lasted. Although they claimed to be Christians, there was no evidence of Christianity in the way they treated each other. They had suffered so much pain and had drifted so far apart that they had become hostile roommates. Their marriage had ended long before they'd begun counseling. We live in a country where the majority of Americans profess to be Christian. This confession often creates confusion when the promises of love aren't supported by lifestyle, when the concept of Christianity is more important than its commitments, when we share the same bed, but lie there together yet alone. It's what happens when we define Christian marriage casually—because how we define marriage determines how we experience marriage.

*It is to look at another person and get a glimpse of
what God is creating, and to say, "I see who God
is making you, and it excites me! I want to be part
of that. I want to partner with you and God in the
journey you are taking to his throne. And when we
get there, I will look at your magnificence and say,
"I always knew you could be like this. I got glimpses
of it on earth, but now look at you!"*
—Timothy Keller

Christian by Default?

Sitting in the airport waiting for a flight, I (Rich) was interested that the man and woman next to me were flying back to India after having been gone for over twenty years. When he found out that I was a pastor, he said, "I too am a Christian!" Before I could respond, he continued explaining that his parents were not Hindu, and in their village, the only other option was Christian. His mother and father found a "Christian holy man" and had him baptized.

"Where do you go to church?"

"Oh, we don't attend church."

"Have you ever been exposed to the teaching of Jesus?"

The long pause answered the question. At that point our flight to London was announced, and we hurried to the gate to find the seat we would be wedged in for the next seventeen hours. I couldn't get out of my mind this man's belief that not being Hindu made him Christian. Yet our nation is filled with people who are Christian by default.

Recently one of our congregation's members shared with me the results from a "man on the street" interview. People walking the streets in a West Coast city were asked to define the term "Christian." Their answers included "a right-wing political party," "a group of fanatics," "an out-of-touch group of people," "individuals who need religion for a crutch," and "religious people." Only one woman identified Christians as people who have accepted Jesus as their Savior.

Our Definition Determines Our Direction

Where we end up in life often depends on how we define key words and concepts. Definitions usually define our direction. Pastor Jim Gleason maintains that "Direction, not desire, determines our destination."[1] That point is so important to Christian marriage. It would even be appropriate to say that definitions and direction determine our destiny—that's where most Christian marriages, like Juanita and Paul's, swerve off the road.

We believe that the Bible teaches that all of mankind, no matter how good we think we are, is under God's judgment. We often use the analogy of being under a guilty verdict with God as the judge of the universe. The verdict requires the death penalty. Instead of our being put to death, Jesus stands before the court and suffers the penalty for us. But death could not hold Him. He lives to guide us and intercede on our behalf. The couple that believes the biblical account of this historical event is "Christian."

Christianity is not a religion that someone can be baptized into; it is a relationship with a living savior. This kind of Christianity weaves its way through the fabric of all of our relationships, especially our marriages. Norman Wright's definition of a Christian marriage can help us here.

Our Definition Determines Our Desire

*A Christian marriage is a total commitment of
two people to the person of Jesus Christ and to one
another. It is a commitment in which there is no*

---

1. Jim Gleason, Corban University chapel, September 30, 2011.

> *holding back of anything. . . . A Christian marriage is similar to a solvent, a freeing up of the man and woman to be themselves and become all that God intends for them to become. Marriage is the refining process that God will use to have us develop into the man or woman he wants us to be.*[2]

This definition highlights four key factors:
- Our first commitment is to Jesus Christ and then to each other.
- Marriage is filled with freedom to express life and love without reservation.
- Married couples don't get lost in the relationship, they get found—they become all they were meant to be.
- Marriage is the "vineyard" that God uses to grow an intoxicating relationship.

I (Rich) struggled with definitions approximately ten years into my marriage. I share my experience in our first book, *Redeeming Relationships.* My struggle, in part, was because I was not totally committed to Jesus Christ and to LouAnna. My definition of marriage minimized her importance. My desire was to be everything I could be, not everything LouAnna needed me to be.

LouAnna was totally committed to Jesus Christ and me. Her definition of a Christian marriage made a huge difference in how we experienced marriage. LouAnna's commitment helped change me. Our marriage grew to reflect the "intoxicating" quality Solomon writes about (Song of Songs 1:2). Our definition of a Christian marriage determines which desires we pursue—and which desires yield fruit in our relationship. Couples who desire to follow what Jesus teaches have more hope of succeeding .

---

2. Wright, H. Norman, Quiet Times for Couples (Eugene, OR: Harvest House Publishers, 2008). 2

Connecting

From the moment we met, we decided that our relationship would be centered on Christ and His will for our lives. As we look back, we realize that this has been the center and source of strength in our marriage.

One of the issues we faced early in our marriage was the tug of war between self-centeredness and other-centeredness. Even though we still face this obstacle from time to time, we have developed a trust in each other that allows us to be vulnerable. Ephesians 4:28–32 has helped keep us on the right path. We ask, is our relationship filled with grace and forgiveness? When we are able to answer this question positively, our marriage remains filled with the love and stability we had at the beginning.

—Eric and Lynn (married 30 years)

Our Definition Determines Our Delight

Dr. Wright is correct when he says that a Christian marriage is "a commitment in which there is no holding back of anything." We have encountered couples whose marriages were characterized by secrecy, pent-up emotions, unresolved conflict, hurt feelings, misunderstandings, guarded love, and lifeless sex. The healthy marriage is vibrant and free. It is free to be honest and open. Hurt feelings are admitted and addressed. There is a feeling that no topic is "off-limits."

We have counseled hundreds of engaged couples. Most of these couples believe marriage will end their individuality, swallow up their identity and that they will become only the spouse of the person they are marrying. The fact is that couples do not lose their individual identities; they add another.

Dr. David Olson, the author of *The Couple Checkup*, asks, "In your relationship is there a good balance of time together and time apart?"[3] The inference drawn from the question is that unhealthy couples define marriage in a way that exhibits an imbalance in this area. The couple that lives separate lives experiences less joy and delight. A healthy couple will spend quality time apart as well as quality time together. This balance promotes a vibrant relationship. How we define our marriage determines the delight we experience in marriage.

Who Defines "Christian Marriage"?

Paul and Juanita saw their differences and struggles with each other as God somehow judging them. They couldn't see that God was using these differences as catalysts for their growth. They missed the truth of Scripture that God was working everything for their good (Romans 8:28) so that they could look like Jesus. Not being able to trust God removed the Christian element from their definition of marriage. Once the incorrect definition was established, and all attempts to change it were disregarded, the relationship disintegrated.

Ultimately, it is the character of our savior that defines the Christian marriage. When the qualities of a self-sacrificing and loving savior are removed from the definition, the relationship not only stops being "Christian"—it stops being a marriage.

---

3. David H. Olson, et. al., The Couple Checkup (Nashville: Thomas Nelson, 2008).

Love Lock: Changing Our Definitions

- Read through Romans 8 and list in a notes app on your phone or on a piece of paper any descriptions of how the paragraphs define those "who are in Christ Jesus." (e.g., 8:1—We are no longer condemned.)

- Read through Song of Songs 8:6–7 and list any descriptions of love (e.g., 8:6— Love is strong like a "seal" over our hearts.)

- Using both lists, compare how the definitions of who we are in Christ from Romans 8 make the love experienced in Song of Songs 8 more achievable.

- Go over the lists each night. They will not only intensify your desire for intimacy, but they will also change your definitions and the direction of your marriage!

I Need to Feel Appreciated and Cherished

Joy, feeling one's own value, being appreciated and loved by others, feeling useful and capable of production are all factors of enormous value for the human soul. —Maria Montessori

CHAPTER 11

Taking the Medicine

I (Rich) have high blood pressure, but I am in constant denial. I take medicine, but deep in my soul I believe that I don't need it. I will drop a few pounds, start walking for forty-five minutes each day, and then stop taking the medicine.

When I take my blood pressure the day after stopping the medicine, my blood pressure is still normal. This confirms my wishful spin: I don't need the medicine. A week later my pressure is still normal, but a little higher than it was before I quit taking the medicine. Two and a half weeks later, my blood pressure is very high, and I stop spinning: I need the medicine. I immediately take a pill and check my pressure the next morning. My pressure is still out of control! Two days later, my pressure is still high, but not as high as it was earlier in the week. It takes several weeks of taking the medicine before my blood pressure finally drops back into the normal range.

There is a medicine designed by God for every Christian. When we take it, it promotes health in every aspect of our lives, especially our marriages. The ingredients of this medicine might sound, at first, as new and exciting as the description on the side of a pill bottle, but once you start taking this medicine, you'll see an increase in the respect you receive.

Ingredient 1: Consistent time in prayer

Dr. Phil (Phillip C. McGraw), in his book *Relationship Rescue*, states:

> *An interesting statistic shared by David McLaughlin in his wonderful series entitled "The Role of the Man in the Family" reflects that the divorce rate in America is at a minimum one out of two marriages. But the reported divorce rate among couples that pray together is about one in ten thousand. Pretty impressive statistic, even if you reduce it a thousand-fold.* [1]

There is something about prayer that not only engages the support and presence of the God who loves us but also increases the intimacy we share as we open our hearts before God and each other.

Ingredient 2: Consistent time in the Bible

The Bible promises to promote health and wellbeing in our lives as we apply its relational insights. Through the Bible we gain wisdom, discretion, and direction in our lives. We should not be surprised that it is an important ingredient in God's prescription for loving someone.

Couples who share their time in the Bible with each other not only learn from the inspired text, but they also develop an appreciation for the self-control it takes to be consistent. That character appreciation promotes respect for each other, increases our desire for intimacy, and sprinkles star dust on our dreams.

---

1. Phillip C. McGraw, Relationship Rescue: A Seven-Step Strategy for Reconnecting with your Partner (New York: Hyperion, 2000), p. 247.

Connecting

We have a consistent time each day when we can talk and pray with each other in a low-stress environment. When deeper issues are on the agenda, we talk while walking side by side instead of staring at each other across the kitchen table.

When our children were small, they'd come too. They would toddle along near us, or we would go to the local park where they could play. As they moved into their teens, we began to leave them at home and simply walk nearby in our neighborhood—a plan that all parties found appealing! During our walks we might turn to prayer. To anyone looking on this just looks like normal conversation, so it doesn't feel strange.

—Rosie and Jim (married 24 years)

Ingredient 3: Consistent time in fellowship

Not long ago one of my friends confessed that he had given up on the church. His thinking was "I'm a member of the universal body of Christ; I don't really need church as much as other Christians."

Ironically, our conversation began with his confession that he had become discouraged with life in general and had stopped appreciating his wife. This scared him and caused him to question the value of his marriage. Without realizing it, he was suffering from not taking the medicine.

The church is the body of Christ into which we have been baptized. Most of the New Testament is a collection of letters sent to local churches where people met and encouraged each other. Church is a place where teaching promotes health and maturity, where authenticity and supportive friendships create a caring community. Without these, Christians grow more slowly and diminish their opportunities to be or feel cherished.

It is in the day-to-day interactions of honest and caring people within our local church that we find our unique connection to other believers. Scripture implies with phrases such as "when one member suffers, we all suffer" that we cannot live authentically without each other. You cannot make it without me, and I cannot make it without you. Our Christian relationships (including marriage) center on being partners with Christ and each other. Our character will never be complete without fellowship with other believers in the context of the local church—and it's complete (mature) character that causes our partner to appreciate and cherish us!

Ingredient 4: Consistent time in service

Every Christian is gifted to serve. Serving is normative in the Christian life and cultivates richness in all of our relationships. Notice the startling statement John makes in his gospel: "He [Jesus] now showed them the full extent of his love" (John 13:1).

Most of us would expect John to write about the crucifixion next—but he doesn't. Why? Isn't Jesus' sacrificial death the best demonstration of the "full extent of his love"? Apparently, the Spirit wanted to communicate something else here, so John writes first about Jesus washing feet. He writes about serving each other. Learning to wash feet adds a healthy dimension to every relationship, especially marriage. How we serve each other in the mundane moments sometimes demonstrates the longevity in our love more readily than the other sacrifices we make.

Little things often demonstrate the larger love. In a sense, we were saved to serve.

When we quit reading the Bible, pray only over meals, avoid engaging in real church friendships, and find serving too time-consuming, we diminish our experience of the delights God created. Over time, our attitudes begin to show the effects of the missing medicine. Our relationships are affected—maybe not the first two days, maybe not even the first two weeks, but our spiritual bloodstream begins to notice the difference.

When a crisis occurs, we pray, but feel that our prayers don't get past the ceiling. We read the Bible, but it doesn't make sense. Church feels like a room full of strangers. It seems like a waste of time—especially when compared to sleeping in!

At this point we're too distracted by our own hurts to know the happiness and health that comes from doing things for others. Like blood pressure medicine, the first pill doesn't usually work on its own; but taking the medicine over time completely changes our condition.

As pastors, our advice to dating couples who want to enjoy a love beyond this world is to stop spinning excuses and begin taking the medicine together. Taking the medicine will provide more insight and wisdom than a weekly visit to your general practitioner. It will change your relationship. It will add authenticity. It will promote meaning. Taking the medicine promotes transformation, and transformed character causes our spouse to cherish us more deeply. It is a prescription for a marriage that is meaningful and magical—in all the right senses of the word.

Love Lock: Taking the Medicine

- Find an empty medicine or lotion bottle.

- Create a prescription about prayer, Bible study, and church attendance. Use your creativity! (e.g., Chews for becoming cherishable, etc.)

- Type or write your creative prescription on a sticker (tape will work) and affix it to the bottle.

- Place the bottle somewhere you frequent each day.

CHAPTER 12

Maturity Matters

J ohn was an angry husband, mostly blind to his behavior. He only had a vague idea of how it affected the people around him—until Cherie pointed it out in a note that cleared his vision fast.

> *"For four years I have put up with your yelling, whining, and complaining. You keep saying you'll try harder, but I don't see any change. I'm sorry, but I'm leaving."*

Now John sat in my (Rich's) car reading the note aloud as we made our way to Cherie's attorney's office. The meeting was short. Cherie wanted to see obvious "evidence of consistent change." It was a "take it or I'm leaving" proposition. For the first time in his marriage, John saw clearly what Cherie had been trying to show him all along—maturity matters.

If you have ever been with children, you realize they are self-absorbed because they are in the center of their own worlds. Children place their pleasures at the center of almost every decision. They find it difficult to appreciate or cherish the relationships they're in. This is normal for a child. It is abnormal for an adult. The apostle Paul reminded his readers that, when he was a child, he talked, thought and reasoned like a child, and that when he grew up, he put "childish ways" behind him (1 Corinthians 13:11). It is this act of putting away that is so difficult. How does a husband, like John, learn to put away childish things?

Learning to Shift

After years of observing college and church couples, we believe movement from immaturity to maturity is characterized by several difficult (and mostly manual) shifts.

- A shift from dependence and independence to interdependence.
- A shift from egocentricity to other-centricity.
- A shift from passivity to proactivity.
- A shift from pleasure-centeredness to purpose-centeredness.
- A shift from the acquisition to the application of knowledge.

First Gear: Shifting to Interdependence

In the progress of personality, first comes a declaration of independence, then a recognition of interdependence. —Henry Van Dyke

When children start maturing, they naturally move from dependency to independence. As they continue to mature, they discover an appreciation of the community around them and become interdependent. The immature, however, are often either dependent on others for their needs or so independent that they become islands in the social sea.

The "one another" passages in the Bible indicate that *interdependence* is something God wants for us. These passages become excellent tools for evaluating our maturity (e.g., John 13:34). Husbands and wives enjoy a more meaningful marriage when they shift to interdependence.

Second Gear: Shifting from Egocentricity to Other-centricity

The immature believe that life is all about them. Their first question every morning is "What can I get out of this day?" It's not unusual for this kind of couple to have conflicts over issues like what movies to watch, what cars to drive, and where to spend their vacations. While mature couples find great pleasure in surprising each other, the immature rarely understand the love-changing benefits of sacrificing an hour each day to add meaning to their marriage—but that's "other-centricity."

Connecting

As we look back on our marriage, we realize that we are a good team. We started our journey committed to local ministry, God's Word and will, and to staying together regardless! We discovered we couldn't put our marriage on auto pilot—it takes a lot of hard work.

One of the practices that helps us strengthen our marriage is our annual checkup. This happens on our anniversary. We spend some quiet, uninterrupted time praying about God's will in our marriage, reviewing our goals, checking to see if we are on the same page, and refocusing on our hopes and vision for the future.

—Michelle and David (married 11 years)

Third Gear: Shifting from Passivity to Proactivity

Many men live passively with wives who are passively waiting for them to figure out how their passivity is affecting the relationship. (That's a lot of passivity!)

Proactivity can be defined as doing the thing that needs doing before it looks like it needs to be done. More than one wife has shared with us how living with a spiritually or emotionally passive man makes her feel less treasured and taken for granted. Men feel the same way about wives whose only interests are cosmetics and clothes.

Men would like their wives to share their hunger for God, to be proactive in lovemaking, and to listen for the feelings they aren't so sure they want to share. Immature couples lack the ability to be proactive because their lack of self-mastery makes them passive, but when a couple shifts this gear, they will also find that proactivity drives pleasure.

Fourth Gear: Sifting from Pleasure to Purpose

The comfort zone is a shrine for adolescents. They refuse to recognize that maturity results from discomfort. Pursuing pleasure is so much easier. To expect instant maturity without any discomfort is like an athlete expecting to be good without any pain—a kind of conflict between the brain and the body. Immaturity pleads with us, "Pain always hurts." Maturity replies, "Sometimes it helps."

Couples who have made this shift handle the discomforts of life together. They've moved past *comfort* through their commitment to each other and have found that discomfort can bring closeness. When *closeness* becomes the purpose rather than maintaining the comfort zone, couples grow.

Fifth Gear: Shifting from Acquiring to Applying

It's not what a person knows that counts. Marriage requires the effective application of our knowledge. We've found that applying what we learn in church, from other successful couples, from sites like StartMarriageRight.com, and from our personal Bible study is not easy. It's easier to coast in neutral, to acquire knowledge rather than manually shift through the gears, but couples who coast seldom enjoy feeling appreciated and cherished.

Immaturity costs couples considerable emotional energy—and as it is with the rest of life, the fuel costs only get higher. Talking through the "shifts" as you attempt to practice them together can help you learn to put each other first, to develop the kind of maturity that encourages you to see each other as more important than other aspects of life. When character matures to that level, couples experience the intimate romance that comes with feeling loved.

Love Lock: Maturity Matters

- Use I Corinthians 13:4–7 and John 13:4–17 to develop a list of important elements in mature love (e.g., patient, kind)

- Talk through the list one element at a time and share with each other a time when you saw that kind of love in your spouse. (It's okay if they demonstrated the part of love to someone else like a child. Talk through those times too).

- Write that time next to the part of love it corresponds to.

- Thank your spouse for showing that kind of love.

- Then take turns choosing an element of love you want to work on for the next week or month. Share that element with your spouse.

- Separately, use your personal calendar to schedule the days you will design practical activities (like foot washing) to show your love to the one you love.

I Need to Trust You

To be trusted is a greater compliment than to be loved. —George MacDonald

CHAPTER 13

Dealing with Damaged Trust

It takes one person to forgive; it takes two
people to be reunited. —Lewis B. Smedes

She sat at the kitchen table fingering the note and staring at yesterday's warmed-over coffee. She replayed her marriage, pausing at scenes that didn't make sense. As she spliced the scenes together, the pattern of Gene's lies began to lay itself out on the oily film in her mug. It seemed so clear now. She focused on a period of several months when the phone rang three or four times a day, but there was never anyone there. She thought it was strange that the caller had blanked out his or her caller ID, but she assumed it was a still just a "wrong number."

She remembered frequently smelling perfume on Gene's suit coats. When she asked, Gene reminded her that his office was filled with women. "My new secretary, Mary, usually puts my coat away for me," he'd suggested. "It must be her perfume."

Beth paused her memory on a day she surprised Gene in his office. She'd almost asked Mary about hanging Gene's coat up but felt guilty about even questioning Gene's honesty.

Beth thought she always gave Gene the benefit of the doubt because she had no reason to question his commitment; now she wondered if she gave him the benefit because she was afraid she'd find what now stared at her from the note in her trembling hand. The note apologized for "the hurt I've caused" and warned that Gene had "been unfaithful" more than a few times. The note was signed, "Sue."

Beth's memory paused at a scene in the mall where a year ago she'd accused him of visually undressing a clerk in Macy's. She was embarrassed and hurt. He again professed his commitment to her but added that "it didn't hurt to look at the menu, even if you were on a diet." She'd never understood that comparison. It made her feel like a salad in a steak house. But, not wanting to create a scene, she'd let it go. She'd let a lot of things go.

Gene came home to his personal belongings thrown into boxes and dumped on the front porch. Taped conspicuously to one of the boxes was Sue's letter to Beth and another note.

"Gene, it's over. Please leave me and the children alone. I called your parents and told them everything. Beth"

Gene was devastated. He had never considered the consequences of Beth finding out. He packed his SUV and sat in the driveway. Tears rolled down his cheeks as the full impact of what he had done sank in.

After three weeks of separation, Gene and Beth agreed to try to save their marriage. They came in for counseling. During the first session, Gene confessed his unfaithfulness and asked Beth for forgiveness. My wife, Linda and I (Marty) watched the transformation. With mercy only God understands, Beth forgave him. After several more weeks of separation, Gene moved back into the home. But, a month later, he sat in my office again.

"I don't believe she's forgiven me," he sighed. I listened as he rehearsed the "inquisition" that "trapped" him—the inquisition I reminded him he'd earned. "I just can't live like this," he countered. "She's always checking up on me. Why can't she for-give me?"

> *Be kind and compassionate to one another, forgiv-*
> *ing each other, just as in Christ God forgave you.*
> Ephesians 4:32

The truth was that Beth had forgiven him, but Gene had con-fused forgiveness with trust. The two are not the same. Two peo-ple can forgive each other without trusting each other. Trust has to be re-earned.

If a couple like Beth and Gene never trust again, the marriage can survive, but it can't thrive. Trust is the catalyst that makes all the emotions and experiences of friendship intense and mean-ingful. Gene was beginning to understand that his wife had for-given him, but too much had happened for her to trust him. He needed to re-earn her trust.

Trust is built one behavior at a time. It will not return unless the one building trust uses the tools of authenticity, honesty, and vulnerability. If we are serious about retooling, trust can remodel the relationship.

> *Without emotional trust, you cannot have*
> *emotional intimacy.* —Mark Goulston

Six Tools for Rebuilding Trust

If your actions have damaged your marriage, these six tools can help you re-establish trust:

- **Chisel your confession.** Confession isn't being sorry you got caught. It's chiseling painfully into stone your admis-sion that the damage was your fault. It's admitting every-thing, not just the things others have already discovered.

- **Hammer out an honest apology.** Be specific about what you did. "I'm sorry I hurt you" doesn't hit the nail on the head. "I damaged your trust when I _____" is honest.

- **Draft a blueprint of what you will change.** If you are apologizing to your spouse, clearly identify how your behavior will change.

- **Hand over the permits.** We need to give the one we've offended permission to check up on all of our words and actions.

- **Relinquish the schedule.** Giving the other person the time he or she needs (or even wants) is the least we can do. The damage was our fault.

- **Miter the martyr.** We need to cut out all attempts to recast events in our favor. It's not about us. It's about the one we've wounded.

Four Tools for Working Toward Forgiveness

It's so easy to allow our justified feelings of betrayal and hurt to morph into a judgmental spirit and related actions. Paul warned us about this. "Do not repay anyone evil for evil. . . . If it is possible, as far as it depends on you, live at peace with everyone. Do not take revenge, my friends, but leave room for God's wrath. . . . 'If your enemy is hungry, feed him; if he is thirsty, give him something to drink' " (Romans 12:17–20).

If you've been hurt by your spouse's actions, these four strategies can help you rebuild your marriage:

- **Forge forgiveness.** Cool your anger quickly. Forgive as Jesus Christ forgave. He didn't make us suffer and sweat before giving us His unconditional forgiveness.

- **Inspect with kindness.** When you inspect the person's honesty, do it with kindness. Avoid rubbing your spouse's face in the mess. It is not necessary that he or she knows each time you check.

- **Measure the progress.** Letting your spouse see how he or she is moving closer on the tape measure of trust will encourage progress.

- **Hand over the tools.** As you begin to see progress, hand over, one at a time, the six tools listed above.

Start Over

Couples we have watched retool their relationships will tell you they feel like they've started all over. They've changed the way they relate to each other and things feel fresh and new. The offending party often experiences a deeper loyalty after being forgiven. When we get to the point where a new, more transparent way of relating is emerging, we need to trash the old sheet rock and particle board—we need to start over.

Rebuilding trust can be time-consuming, like remodeling a home stud by stud. But, although it sounds one-dimensional, the result is often three-dimensional, and usually better than the original. Couples we have worked with over our combined sixty years of ministry can tell you firsthand that trust can be restored. Our prayer is that you won't give up and that you'll follow the blueprints inspired by our Creator.

Ultimately, like any satisfying building project, you get what you pay for. The price here is forgiveness and a willingness to rebuild the trust that was damaged. Those two sacrifices will not only reflect the will of the Master Carpenter, but they'll also redeem your relationship.

Love Lock: Blowing in the Wind

- Using a pencil and 3×5 card or other heavyweight paper, list something you appreciate about your spouse's character.

- Now, retrace over the top of that aspect of character three times so the words are dark and deep.

- Next, softly write a word or phrase that represents something that you believe has diminished some of the joy in your relationship (e.g. self-centeredness, ungratefullness, tardiness, etc.).

- Finally, erase the softly written word or phrase and blow the bits of eraser onto the floor.

- Ask God to help you chisel into stone (metaphorically) those things that bring delight and blow away those things that need to be forgiven.

CHAPTER 14

Come Out of the Cold!

*It's so important to keep a marriage alive with
small treats and doing little things for each other.
Just remembering to say nice things and to have
listening time is vital. That ghastly phrase 'quality
time' means taking three minutes to sit down and
be still with someone rather than yelling over your
shoulder as you rush out.* —Joanna Lumley

We've all heard the maxim "When life gives you lemons, make lemonade." Ever tried it? It'll make your heart pucker! That's because lemonade made from squeezing life into a glass just tastes like the sour life it was squeezed from. You have to add something sweet to make the maxim (and life) work.

But comparisons can help us think from another point of view, so the lemonade maxim does work at some level. In view of that fact, maybe there's a metaphor that can help us with the icy frost that sometimes blasts through our marriages. Maybe there's a way of looking at the cold created by conflict that might help us reduce the chill! How about this idea? (Okay, get ready for the ridiculous—for the moment anyway):

When Marriage Gives You Ice, Build an I.G.L.O.O.

Wait! Before you go back to scraping snow off the windshield of your spouse's heart, the acrostic actually makes a helpful outline for resolving conflict. Here's how it works:

I—Invest time and energy

- **Increase deposits.** No matter how "happily-ever-afterish" or "hellish" our marriages might seem, investing in the relationship is the right strategy. Marriages improve when we invest in the words and actions that created happiness in the first place.

    > *An Emotional Bank Account is a metaphor*
    > *that describes the amount of trust that's*
    > *been built up in a relationship. It's the feel*
    > *ing of safeness you have with another*
    > *human being.* —Stephen Covey

    Before we try to resolve conflict, we must ensure that we're still making emotional bank deposits. Enjoying the strong sense of trust that a marriage can offer is less promising when the other person feels like there's more leaving the account than coming in. Even in a bone-chilling marriage, investing time and energy is the right approach. Rich and I have watched many couples start rebuilding trust as soon as they do something nice for the one they love.

- **Learn each other's needs.** Paul instructed the early church to build people up "according to their needs" (Ephesians 4:29). Paul's wisdom helps us in marriage too. At the beginning of our marriages, most of us are uncomfortable with failure. We avoid helpful questions like, "Am I meeting your needs?" We find it easier to hope and pretend that the communication climate is tropical when it may not be. Learning to meet each other's needs can keep the ice from forming, replacing it with the warmth of a love that says, "If I'm not meeting your needs, I want to know, because I care more about you than I do about my success as a spouse."

G—Glue the rug down

We've all been told that you can't "sweep things under the rug"—but we try to do it anyway. One class period, when I was asking my students why hiding our hearts is unwise, one of my freshmen, Kevin Straw, replied, "Because if you keep sweeping things under the rug, the door won't open."

I paused class for a moment and complimented his level of understanding. Then I asked him for permission to quote him. If we walk into conflicts caused by broken trust with this kind of wisdom, we'll smack into fewer closed doors.

- **Don't "spin" your sin.** It's tempting to rewrite history so we can come out looking a bit more righteous. But, this kind of manipulation stalls resolution, because it affects our spouse's view of our character. We might compare spinning our sin to the delirious aftereffects of spinning around in circles blindfolded. Take off the blindfold, turn us loose, and we can't walk straight. We've damaged the equilibrium in the environment and we need to admit it. Paul reminds us to "put off falsehood and speak truthfully" (Ephesians 4:25). When we approach a conflict with complete honesty, we keep the rug down and the door open.

L—Lose the attitude

- **Rehearse and visualize what you plan to say.** Choose your words and tone carefully. You may want to write both down. How you say something is as important as what you say. Rehearsing and visualizing can help you start with the right attitude.

- **Don't throw snowballs.** Bringing up a conflict as part of another conversation only shows your spouse you can't control yourself. Resolution works best when it is the focus of its own meeting. No one likes to be blindsided by a snowball in the middle of an unrelated, or only slightly-related, conversation.

O—Own your behavior

The Bible details the behaviors God honors: those actions that lead to self-control, humility, peace, harmony, sympathy and love. Use this list of behaviors to help you determine how you are going to respond before you confront. If necessary, visualize how a mature person would handle such a situation and play that role. Here are some helpful ideas:

- **Pray for sunshine.** Before we engage in resolution, we should pray for creativity, courage, an open door, maturity, and wisdom. We also recommend praying with your spouse. (Although this can "feel" patronizing at first, if you follow through with the prayer, God will too.) When we pray, God helps us with the weather.

- **Find the right time.** I (Rich) still remember the day I was supposed to be dropping my daughters at their middle school at 8:15 a.m. so that I could make an 8:30 meeting.

Instead, I sat in the driveway loading my emotional canon. Finally, the doors flew open, and two happy, energetic girls slid into the backseat. As we pulled out of the driveway, I started blasting away,

"Every day this goes on, and I'm getting tired of it. When you make me late, I start my meetings late. This makes everyone late for the entire day." I waved a hand in the air for effect; then I looked in the rearview mirror only to see my youngest crying.

"What's *your* problem?" I growled. My oldest daughter answered instead.

"You know what your problem is, Dad? You don't listen to yourself. You travel all over teaching about conflict resolution and the importance of timing . . . well this is a lousy time to bring this up."

She was right. Most of us treat broken trust as an emergency, but rarely do we encounter a conflict situation that is. We should avoid resolving conflicts on the way to school or work, at the table, just before bed—or when one of the participants is running late.

- **Define the problem without personalizing.** It's important to avoid using "you" statements. Define the problem in writing before the meeting. Your note cards should include your contribution to the problem, your feelings about it, how you think your spouse sees the problem, what you agree on, and what behaviors would contribute to a solution. Although moving toward the "facts" won't guarantee a peaceful resolution, it is the right approach.

- **Identify alternative solutions.** In a recent meeting with city planners, I (Rich) experienced the advantage of an alternative solution. Our church had been debating how to fund the purchase of additional land for parking. The city planner suggested that if we change our paradigm from a suburban church to a city church, we could save land and money. He said, "What if you do what churches in New York City do and sell a small piece of your existing property to a retailer who would build a multiple story parking garage? The retailer would use the parking during the week and you would use it on evenings and Sundays." If we spend time identifying alternative solutions in our marriages, we may find a little more room for "parking."

- **Decide on a mutually acceptable solution.** When you believe you have a workable resolution, ask, "Does it include practical steps that will actually solve the problem for both of us?" A mutually acceptable resolution places the conflict in a new context and melts some of the ice.

  Some relationships are bitterly cold because one partner refuses to work on the problem even though the other partner is ready and willing. This kind of relational difficulty requires outside help—someone who can convince your spouse of the cost-benefit in repairing your relationship.

O—Open your heart to forgiveness

> *Be kind and compassionate to one another, forgiving each other, just as in Christ God forgave you.*
> Ephesians 4:32

The ice only melts completely when we learn to forgive. Christ's example does more than inspire us in this: It teaches us how to forgive. Every conflict, like every sin, requires forgive-ness. Sometimes it's an easier forgiveness—"you washed my white socks with a red what?" It's fairly easy to forgive this kind of offense, but without forgiveness, even this little infraction be-gins to bleed into the friendship, touching every other part of the relationship with its color. The serious conflicts, like the times we wound each other with our words, take longer to resolve. Jesus's example reminds us that sacrifice is part of forgiveness—giving up a "right" to right a wrong. Here are some guidelines that can help us open our hearts to forgiveness:

- **Try to understand** the pain in your spouse's background. The sacrifice of time in this area produces warmth in ev-ery other area of a marriage. There is something compel-ling about understanding each other, about forgiving each other, about putting a warm blanket of words around the one we love.

- **Forgive** even when hate "feels" right and justified. That's what kindness and compassion are all about. Jesus for-gave us precisely when the salary for our sin was death (Romans 3:23). Resolving conflict means following His example; it means bringing warmth to our marriages by trading the high-handed demand for justice with the nail-scarred hands of forgiveness.

A simple acrostic like I.G.L.O.O can help us think through principles that discourage the icy chill. When my oldest son was five years old, he curled up on the living room floor one Saturday morning and began role-playing a scene from a cartoon. "I'm all alone in this cold, cruel world," he repeated over and over. Chris, his two-year-old brother, with his favorite blanket in tow, entered the room and watched, unaware that his brother was acting out a cartoon. As he listened, tears formed. He dropped his blanket, ran to his brother and said, "You can stay in my house!"

Isn't that what love says? When the friendship grows cold and the chill-factor seems unbearable, mature love drops what it's doing, runs across the room, and says, "You can stay in my house!"

Love Lock: Warming the Chill

While praying for an opportunity to add warmth to your relationship, try one of the following:

1. Select a card that helps you thank your spouse for a recent moment when he or she chose to "glue the rug down." Feel free to mention details about how keeping concerns or issues out in the open strengthened your feelings of connection.

2. Start by wearing something that might encourage your spouse to want to "dance" with you. As you enter the room, mention how much "losing the attitude" promoted feelings of closeness. Then dance close!

I Need More Resolution, Less Conflict

The most common mistake couples make while trying to resolve conflicts is to respond before they have the full picture. This inevitably leads to arguments. When people respond too quickly, they often respond to the wrong issue. —Gary Chapman

CHAPTER 15

Shruggers

Problem-Solvers and Rescuers can ruin a marriage. For these personality types, every conflict feels like an opportunity for Sherlock to grab his magnifying glass and root out the offending party. Even ordinary circumstances like discovering exploded eggs in the microwave or finding a Lego in your USB port become time-consuming cases.

Most marriages are benefitted by a shared understanding that not all conflicts should become cases for interrogation—not all conflicts are ours to fix. Marty and I have found over the past thirty years of counseling that those with personalities bent toward rescue and problem-solving often miss important clues for conflict resolution.

Is This a Conflict I'm Supposed to Solve?

If we want to reduce relational conflicts, we need to learn to ask one question, "Is this a conflict I'm supposed to solve?" God doesn't expect us to do anything about some potential conflicts—they are what we call "shruggers." For example, the Shrugger is what King Solomon had in mind when he wrote, "Like one who seizes a dog by the ears is a passer-by who meddles in a quarrel not his own" (Proverbs 26:17).

Although this example involves conflicts between other individuals, it presents an important principle to Problem-Solvers and Rescuers: seizing every conflict by the ears isn't wise.

Meddling in a quarrel when we should shrug can create painful results, but it's the kind of thing we often do. Like a stubborn case of static-cling, every testy situation ends up sticking to us. We grimace, knowing we are about to grab another dog by the ears, but even anticipating the pain isn't enough to make us let go. Instead of evaluating the situation and shrugging, we apply the death grip. And after all is said and done, we wonder, "What went wrong?"

Most marriages can be benefitted by learning to shrug. The apostle Paul gives us some practical counsel:

> *Carry each other's **burdens**, and in this way you will fulfill the law of Christ. If anyone thinks he is something when he is nothing, he deceives himself. Each one should test his own actions. Then he can take pride in himself, without comparing himself to somebody else, for each one should carry his own* **load.** Galatians 6:2–5 (emphasis added)

The word *burdens* commonly refers to something that is too heavy to carry alone. It must be carried by two or more people. The word *load* in verse 5 refers to something carried by one person. When our spouses are struggling with burdens, Paul is implying that we must wisely determine which burden or load they have. Is this a burden too great for them to carry or is this a load they must bear alone? When it is the latter, our response should not be to carry the load for them, but to come alongside and help them discover the skills and wisdom they need to carry the "load" themselves. This concept is especially difficult for Problem-Solvers and Rescuers.

Problem-Solvers

If you find it difficult to listen to a problem without diving in with a sure fix, you may not have learned how to shrug. The solution is to realize that some problems have a divine purpose—and that purpose might be to help the person who has the problem. Failing to shrug can create new problems and delay the maturity that comes from learning to fix our own mistakes.

Sixty combined years of working with people have taught us that when we fail to shrug, we often make a mess of situations that were never ours to mess with in the first place. We've also learned that people need to struggle sometimes to solve their own problems. If we learn to shrug and let them struggle, they can mature. If we fail to shrug, we can hold them back from becoming the best people they can be. With a little listening and some encouragement, people will often take the right steps on their own. That's another reason it's important that we learn to shrug.

Rescuers

Many husbands and wives spend their waking moments looking for ways to rescue the people they love. Motivated by compassion and the good feelings associated with helping others, these spouses are usually unaware that letting go of the dog's ears may be the best avenue of growth. Sometimes they can't let go because they've become co-dependent on helping the people they love.

Angela was this kind of person. Her husband, Tim, had been investigated because of anger issues in the workplace. Twice her pastors and I (Marty) had advised her to support the company's request that he attend anger management classes. However, she could not bear the thought of his suffering the embarrassment and twice decided to rescue him by "re-framing" and "justifying" anger episodes she had observed in their home. Tim, in fact, knew that his wife would come to his rescue (partly to protect her own longing for a "perfect" marriage). So Tim continued to live an outwardly healthy but inwardly troubled life.

Finally, after an angry confrontation with one of their children, Angela expressed her concerns to Tim and her pastors. After six months of counseling, the not-so-perfect marriage has become an authentic testimony of real marriage—a relationship full of God's amazing grace and healing.

Rescuers usually "feel" like they're doing the right thing, but when they fail to ask the right questions, they slow down the healing process and add the stress of failed rescue attempts to their growing caseloads.

In their best-selling book, *Boundaries*, Dr. Cloud and Dr.Townsend warn:

> *Made in the image of God, we were created to take responsibility for certain tasks. Part of taking responsibility, or ownership, is knowing what is our job, and what isn't. Workers who continually take on duties that aren't theirs will eventually burn out. It takes wisdom to know what we should be doing and what we shouldn't. We can't do everything.*[1]

When we learn to shrug, we help our spouses learn to carry their own loads—and we learn the joy and freedom of carrying our own loads, as well. When we shrug, everyone wins. The next time your spouse begins experiencing a difficulty, before you jump in, ask, "Is this a shrugger?" The answer to this question will take our inner Sherlock out of the game and save our marriages from the associated costs.

----

1. Henry Cloud and John Townsend, *Boundaries: When to Say Yes, How to Say No to Take Control of Your Life* (Grand Rapids: MI, Zondervan, 1992), 25.

Love Lock: Learning to Shrug

- The next time you face a conflict in your relationship, ask God, "Do you have purpose for me in helping resolve this, or is this a burden my partner needs to learn from?"

- Then, make a list of possible lessons your spouse might learn from solving the problem with God's help (not yours).

- Next, pray about the best time to share the list with your partner.

- If your partner doesn't see your perspective and wants you to bear a burden that does not seem like yours to bear, agree to meet with a staff member at church.

- Finally, if it was appropriate to shrug and you did, look for any growth in your spouse's life and celebrate what you find! (Write a note, schedule a celebratory date, etc.)

CHAPTER 16

The War of Two Worlds

The minute I (Rich) hear the words of the old spiritual, "This World Is Not My Home," the melody moves from my head to my foot, and it starts tapping to the rhythm. J. R. Baxter's song captures a biblical truth: This isn't home for us. As a kid, this song made sense to me in a sentimental way. Growing up, I believed its message but began to feel instead like "Harry" in the Eagles hit song, "New York Minute," who one day "crossed some line" and was "too much in this world."

When I came out of college, I was ready to make my mark in health care, but ten years later, I looked around and realized that I had crossed that line and "was too much in this world." I had a great job, a spacious home, a good church, a Porsche—I thought I had it all. Through a series of events motivated by my love affair with the world, I faced losing my wife and family. A conversation with my pastor helped me realize I was at war with two worlds: the one on earth and the other in heaven. It was destroying my relationships. Worldliness does that.

This is the war that Andrea and Mike are battling as they pay bills in their study. Tension packs the room as they revisit the enormity of their financial problem. Mike works as a middle manager in a growing high-tech company. But, after five years there, his $90,000 annual salary isn't enough to cover their expenses.

Andrea works part-time. She can't work anymore without robbing time from their two young boys. Half of what she earns goes toward paying for day care. Tonight is no different from all of the other taxing "bill nights." Mike says they're struggling because Andrea has a Macy's in her closet. She says it's more like a JC Penney from the last decade. She reminds him that playing golf is an expensive luxury. He defends his golf expenses as a good business move.

When all of their bills are combined, they are $300 a month short. In the past, they refinanced their house to make up the difference. They now have no equity left, even though the house is worth nearly $200,000 more than the $650,000 they paid. Each month they put the $300 on a credit card. (They're accumulating air miles, but they can't afford to go anywhere.)

The solution temporarily resolves the cash flow problem, but the weight never leaves. They feel like all they're doing is switching heavy luggage from one hand to the other while hurrying through the airport of life. They discuss changing banks to get a lower interest rate. But, Mike and Andrea know they need to switch more than hands and banks; they need to switch worlds.

Set your minds on things above, not on earthly things. Colossians 3:2

Even though they are making more money than their parents ever made, they fight more and laugh less. Their financial frenzy has damaged their respect for each other so the tenderness is gone. Their two sons listen to emotional outbursts almost every night. They've learned to yell at each other and crave new toys just like Mom and Dad. Mike and Andrea's unwillingness to get rid of the country club membership and replace their new BMW with an economical second car is motivated by questions like, "What would people think?" That kind of question results from losing what we call, "the war of the worlds."

*Dear friends, I urge you, as aliens and strangers in
the world, to abstain from sinful desires, which war
against your soul.* 1 Peter 2:11

According to the Center for American Progress:

- The average American family's debt has increased over 30 percent since 2001. It presently stands at 117.6 percent of income.

- Approximately 13.5 percent of the families surveyed have debt-service expenses (monthly payments) that average 40 percent of their income.

- Families are having a hard time keeping up in the current economic climate.[1] The problem is exacerbated by fast cash and credit cards. What we want, we can buy . . . because our debt is invisible—until it ruins our relationships.

*"Life is more than food, and the body more than
clothes."* Luke 12:23

Too Much in This World

It is a complicated picture. This world system presents a standard of living that is far beyond the average person's means to achieve. The standard drags us beneath the surface of an unmerciful ocean of discontent whose relentless waves pound against the shores of our sanity, repeating "more, more, more." We become depressed, and all hope for redeeming relationships damaged by this world's values sinks beneath waves of despair.

---

1. The Center for American Progress. www.americanprogress.org

The Eagles capture this melancholic depression in their song "New York Minute." The song tells of a Wall Street broker, "Harry," whose clothing was found "scattered somewhere on the track." The song reminds us that men "get lost sometimes" and die because they live "too much in this world." It's a powerful reminder of what the apostle John meant when he said:

> *If anyone loves the world, the love of the Father is not in him. For everything in the world—the cravings of sinful man, the lust of his eyes and the boasting of what he has and does—comes not from the Father but from the world. The world and its desires pass away, but the man who does the will of God lives forever.* 1 John 2:15–17

War Wounds

John describes four wounds that pierce our relationships. First, we do not "love" God. Second, we "crave" more. Third, we "lust" after what we see around us. And fourth, we "boast" about what we have. Understanding these wounds helps us understand why any one of us can find ourselves on the same spreadsheet as Andrea and Mike.

Love's Lost

When we are "too much in this world," we miss out on fulfilling the joy of our created purpose. We miss out on the one relationship that makes all our relationships truly redemptive. If "the love of the Father is not in us," we won't have it to add warmth and meaning to our relationships, and we won't have it to help us heal the hurt of relationships damaged by a love of the world. What Andrea and Mike started with was every young person's hope for "real love." They never would have dreamed that their attraction could be turned from each other to a world of designer clothes, diamonds, and distractions.

Connecting

In a Media course that we took together while we were still dating, we talked about how ads that sell products based on the convenience they provide can cause us to value convenience more that we probably should—so much that when our friendships become inconvenient for even a short period of time, we abandon them.

Roger and I were surprised by this and decided that along with regular media fasts, we would discuss any ads or movie themes we thought might influence our relationship. We're thankful for these deeper conversations and for the closeness they've created in our friendship, but we're still working to make sure the world doesn't become more important to us than our love for God or for each other. —Elaine and Roger (married 8 years)

Curbing the Cravings

Unfortunately, through a phenomenon educators call "transference," we've learned to treat our relationships the way we treat products. We carry over what we learn about consuming in our market economy into our friendships and relationships with family members, coworkers and employees. It becomes easy for us to focus our energies on what we crave rather on what we can give. We crave a product; we crave a relationship. It just makes sense to us.

But people aren't products. In a sense, the more we buy into this kind of lifestyle, the more we sell out on every relationship we have. How do we curb the cravings?

In my (Marty's) Media and Society class, the students explore the contrast between the worldview that says life is about consuming and the Scriptures that teach that life is about adoring God and giving to others. The goal is that along with identifying the underlying media theories, the students will learn to examine the effects the "war of the worlds" has on who they have become. The discussion is designed to help students understand how *adoration* helps protect us from discontentment while *giving* protects us from the power of our cravings.

Because the following exercise allows you to focus on any aspect of the "war of the worlds," the same process can be used to win our war against envy, pride, lust, slander, gossip, etc. Mike and Andrea followed this counsel, and their relationship began to improve—but it wasn't easy. Powerful cultural influences continued to haunt their efforts, as they do ours.

After over sixty combined years of ministry, we're both convinced: The way to avoid becoming like Mike and Andrea or "Harry" in the Eagles's song is to live outside the "New York Minute"—to live and love beyond this world.

Love Lock: Winning the War

The following exercise can help you change the frequency of conflicts caused by being "too much in this world."

1. Divide a piece of paper, restaurant napkin, or a notetaking screen on your phone into two columns.

2. In the first column, write a list of things you "crave" about God and the life He's given you. At the end of each item put a number representing how many years (approximately) you believe you have valued each item.

3. In the second column, list any reoccurring relational conflicts. Try to list them next to the item in the middle column that contrasts most with your area of relational conflict.

4. Study the lists and ask God to create cravings for those things that provide eternal satisfaction.

CHAPTER 17

Get Invited!

I argue very well. Ask any of my remaining friends.
I can win an argument on any topic, against any
opponent. People know this, and steer clear of me
at parties. Often, as a sign of their great respect,
they don't even invite me. —Dave Barry

Unlike like the humorist Dave Barry, most of us *want* to be invited to the party. Most of us want to be the kinds of people others enjoy being around. We want to sail through life cheering people on to love and good deeds, encouraging their dreams and leading them around the buoys of disappointment. What we *don't want* is to be the person who comes crashing down on their party like a sneaker wave. After all, we tell ourselves we're made for riding waves, not making them. Often when we see conflict grinding in like an Oregon swell, we run for higher ground—to statements like "Real love doesn't confront, it forgives"; "My relationships can succeed without confrontation"; "It's easier to put up with conflict."

We've read the books and met the people. Some suggest that the best way to handle conflict is to adopt one strategy you can use for all situations—a one-size-fits-all approach. Unfortunately, just like those clothes that don't often fit (and leave much to be desired in the shape department), the one-size conflict clothes don't wear well either.

Some Things to Purge from Your Closet:

- Deny it
  Some of us grew up with the following kind of thinking:

  *Conflict is simply a matter of overemphasizing
  your culture's or church's stereotypes. If you don't
  acknowledge it, it can't affect you.*

  Just ask Marge and Nathan if that statement is true. They chanted their way into this strategy of denial almost forty years ago. And their conflicts have been minimal it seems—at least to them. Ask their children and friends, however, and it's a matter of mistaken identity.

  Marge and Nathan don't get along. But, like an alcoholic who can "stop whenever he wants," their relational conflict shows up everywhere except in their own heads. Their kids see it. Their few remaining friends see it, but Marge and Nathan deny its existence. Along with the hurt they create in the people around them, individuals who deny their conflicts enjoy less meaningful relationships and experience less life satisfaction. They live less. They diminish the rewards of relationships because they cannot redeem a brokenness that isn't "real."

- Give in
  Some of us just give in when faced with conflict. People around us even encourage our "go with the flow" attitude when we let them have their way. Some of the time our areas of relational conflict are not important—like who

chooses the next movie. But when a potentially difficult conflict arises, we pay an emotional price if we give in. Over time, our "give-in" attitude just plain gives out, and we become resentful and bitter.

- Stuff it

We've all lived, played, or worked with stuffers. When asked how they "feel," they go silent. Since it takes considerable emotional energy to share their feelings, they stuff them. They expect people to read their minds. Over time, they become angry and bitter—especially if our ESP is DOA.

- Work it

The solutions that emerge from this approach are more about gaining some and losing little than about finding the best solution. The problem with working a deal is that the results may be based upon salesmanship (think "House of Representatives") where hidden agendas win the day but discourage relationships tomorrow. With this strategy, people walk away placated, only to realize later that very little changed.

- Play it

In ice hockey, when a member of a team fouls a member of the opposing team, the player who committed the foul spends time in the penalty box. Then the other team has a one-person advantage called the "power play." Because the penalized team is one player short, the other team tries to take advantage of the situation.

When we use this approach in conflict management, we are usually trying to set up the conflict resolution situation so that we have an advantage. Instead of letting the other person use all his or her players (like the place we meet, the topics we allow, the time of day, the evidence we reject), we use the power play so that we have more players on the ice. But the problem with resolving conflict with this approach is that it never redeems the relationship—it never gets off the ice.

True Resolution

True resolution requires a servant's heart, a loving manner, a listening ear, and an openness to communicate effectively. It takes maturity—and that's, partly, a head skill. When we value the people in our relationships, we seek to resolve our conflict, because resolution produces not only more joy in our relationships, but it also grows us up into better people.

Many of the statistics about divorce imply that unresolved conflict is the biggest reason for the majority of divorces in America. The time to begin working on resolving conflict is when the friendship begins. When we decide to resolve our conflicts rather than winning, we are saying that we value the other person while maintaining the need to meet our own needs.

This concept is what Peter wanted us to understand when he wrote to husbands. "Husbands, in the same way be considerate as you live with your wives, and treat them with respect as the weaker partner and as heirs with you of the gracious gift of life, so that nothing will hinder your prayers" (I Peter 3:7).

The words *respect* and *partner* and the phrase "heirs with you of the gracious gift of life" communicate the precious nature of our marriages. They also remind us that conflict resolution requires them—respect, partnership and a shared perspective. When we enter the storms of conflict, we need to be mindful of these three words. Taking them to heart and considering them in our heads can help us reduce the frequency of relational conflict and promote a deeper and stronger connection—and that's how you get invited to the party!

Love Lock: Party On!

This is a personal activity (at first), so choose a quiet place where you can turn off any electronic devices and spend time praying, writing down your answers, and working through the following:

1. Do my decisions clearly communicate to my spouse that she/he is a valued partner in our decision-making? (Try to write out a recent time when you heard or sensed your spouse feel valued in a decision the two of you made.)

2. Does my spouse "deeply sense" that I see myself as a co-heir of the "gracious gift of life"?

3. Get back together and share your answers.

4. Now, celebrate the positive examples seen in your love for each other—in whatever way you prefer—but decide together!

CHAPTER 18

Contentment's Kiss

I am a wall, and my breasts are like towers.
Thus I have become in his eyes like one
bringing contentment. Song of Songs 8:10

In her recent best-seller, *Hi, Anxiety: Life with a Bad Case of Nerves*, Kat Kinsman, a self-described "professional anxiousologist," shares how the happiness in her marriage helps reduce her anxiety and promote peace.[1] Three thousand years ago, the Scriptures presented the same enduring truth: wise couples encourage an atmosphere and attitude of rest.

The NIV's translation of "contentment" in Song of Songs 8:10 originates from the familiar Hebrew term, "shalom." The writer's point seems to be that the bride's (or Lady Wisdom's) mature, sensitive character ("I am a wall") and her celebrated intimacies ("my breasts are like towers") diminished the anxieties they experienced and brought peace into their marriage.

Just as the "walls" and "towers" of the ancient cities had little to do with their size and more with how they welcomed weary

---

1. Kat Kinsman, *Hi, Anxiety: Life with a Bad Case of Nerves* (New York: Dey Street Books, 2016).

and anxious travelers, aspects of our character and the intoxicating intimacies in our marriages welcome our spouses into a relationship characterized by rest. We could summarize it this way: character and closeness promote peace.

Wise couples encourage an atmosphere of rest.

A thousand years after the Song of Songs, Jesus told an audience, "Come to me, all you who are weary and burdened, and I will give you rest. Take my yoke upon you and learn of me, for I am gentle and humble in heart, and you will find rest for your souls" (Matthew 11:28–29).

His words demonstrate how much stress and anxiety still plagued His creation. Those religious institutions that should have proffered peace had instead yoked their followers to lists of angst-inducing rules. Combine those feelings of not measuring up with the pressures derived from the worldly ambitions His people waded through each day, and all of us can appreciate the gentleness in Jesus's words. Jesus's character and the intoxicating closeness His coming to earth created, welcomed humanity into a relationship of rest. "For I am gentle and humble in heart, and you will find rest for your souls" (Matthew 11:29).

In the two thousand years since Jesus said this, the need for rest has not changed. Combine this historical insight with Alex Williams's conclusion that we may be entering "a new Age of Anxiety," and one thing becomes obvious: our marriages need shalom more than ever.[2]

---

2. Alex Williams, "The Prozac Nation Is Now the United States of Xanax," *The New York Times*, June 10, 2017, https://www.nytimes.com/2017/06/10/style/anxiety-is-the-new-depression-xanax.html.

Connecting

It was entirely my fault! But, to be fair, I really didn't know what I was doing. My military training had taught me the value of planning out every move and becoming as efficient as possible—that's what deeply hurt our marriage.

My constant comments, "Wouldn't this make more sense?" "What if we did it this way, instead?" and the infamous, "Why do you think that?" made my husband feel like he was "walking on" the proverbial eggshells. Every move he made was being evaluated by an efficiency judge—me!

When our pastor spoke about the importance of "shalom," I knew my husband was not experiencing it in our marriage. So, we started talking about what motivated my comments, and I learned a few replacement phrases that worked for him. This has taken us a few years, but it has drawn us closer. —Carolyn and Eddie (married 7 years)

So how do we promote the benefits of the "walls" and the "towers" that Solomon described? Rich and I suggest exploring at least two questions:

#1: Do my words produce rest?

Jesus said that when we "learn" from Him, we enter a state of rest deep within—a soul rest. Throughout the New Testament,

His judicious words brought this kind of peace. In *Loving Your Neighbor: Surprise! It's Not What You Think*, David Sanford skillfully navigates even the "harsh" words Jesus sometimes used and shows the "loving" intent buried in these expressions.[3] The point is that even Jesus's most difficult words promoted shalom. The question is, do mine?

In order to proffer this kind of peace, we need to turn off the distractions and reflect on our relationship. After some moments of reflection, sometimes I (Marty) have to apologize to my wife because I can tell that the words or tone I chose increased her anxiety or stress. Other times I don't notice, and she has to tell me. Either way, without this honest reflection and conversation, I cannot encourage the kind of rest Jesus modeled. I cannot provide the kind of atmosphere Linda deserves.

#2: Do my expectations promote rest?

Leo and Angie had been married for almost ten years and found themselves agitated and anxious. Leo's mom had kept a spotless house, and he was irritated that his was a mess. I (Rich) asked Leo, "Did your mom work outside the home?" He fidgeted with his watch.

"She was a homemaker."

I explained to Leo that his expectation, not Angie's character, was creating the angst he was experiencing. I suggested they clean the house together once a week. Once Leo realized this expectation was creating distance in their relationship and weakening the love they experienced, he began to look at other expectations. This simple practice helped strengthen their marriage. Why? Because shared expectations encourage rest.

---

3. David Sanford, *Loving Your Neighbor: Surprise! It's Not What You Think* (Portland, OR: David Sanford, 2017.)

When your soul is resting, your emotions are okay,
your mind is okay, and Your will is at peace with
God, not resisting what He's doing. —Joyce Meyer

The more our environments promote anxiety and stress, the more time we will need to spend promoting rest. Partners who work with difficult people or who grew up in perfectionistic families need extra sensitivity in this area. Sharing our expectations in compassionate conversations can help our spouses understand what it is we desire in and from the marriage relationship.

That shared understanding is part of what creates the strength in human love—part of what the Author of Love describes in the *Song of Songs*. If we subscribe to His wisdom, we can sing with the female lead and become in our lover's eyes "like one bringing contentment." The relational peace, experienced together day after day, will inspire a deeper and stronger friendship—the kind of friendship that makes us want to walk out onto the bridge, *lock our love*, and throw away the key.

Love Lock: Contentment's Kiss

The following is patterned after an activity described by the Spirit of God in chapters 4:1–7 and 5:10–16 of the Song of Songs.

- Take your spouse somewhere you like to go for romance, face each other, and hold hands.

- Starting at each other's heads (see Song of Songs 4:1–7 and 5:10–16), take turns thanking each other for the contentment that each part of the person brings into your life. (e.g. "Your creative mind makes me smile," "Your eyes are like [use a favorite bird metaphor here. Solomon uses "doves."]; they bring comfort.")

- Continue this activity until you reach each other's feet (if you get that far!) or you can move the opposite direction like the couple does in 7:1–9.

All God's Best!

We hope these chapters will encourage the "strengthening" of your love, so that you will be able to sing with the Song of Songs' lovers:

> *Place me like a seal over your heart, like a seal on*
> *your arm; for love is as strong as death, its ardor*
> *unyielding as the grave. It burns like blazing fire,*
> *like the very flame of the Lord. Many waters cannot*
> *quench love; rivers cannot wash it away. If one were*
> *to give all the wealth of his house for love, it would*
> *be utterly scorned.* Song of Songs 8:6–7

With blessing, Rich and Marty

About the Authors

Rich Rollins, DMin, has served as a health care professional, college vice president, pastor, and church consultant. He presently serves as an adjunct faculty member at Corban University's School of Ministry in Salem, Oregon. For more than forty years, Rich's work in pastoral leadership and church organizations has made him a sought-after consultant and conference speaker. Rich and his wife, LouAnna, have been married for more than fifty-five years. Their two married daughters, two sons-in-law, three grandchildren, and two foster daughters all encourage Rich in his ministry and appreciation of golf, reading, and sports.

Rich is the coauthor of *Redeeming Relationships* and *Spiritual Fitness* and also codirects Redeemingrelationships.com.

Marty Trammell, PhD, is the English Chair at Corban University and a pastor at Valley Baptist Church. Nicknamed "Dr. Love" by his students and colleagues, Marty enjoys sharing premarital counseling and speaking ministries with his wife and best friend, Linda. He speaks regularly at retreats and conferences and has contributed study notes to various Bibles and books. Marty and Linda have three sons, two daughters-in-law, and three grandchildren who encourage their love and help them enjoy music, sports, camping, and road trips.

Marty is the coauthor of *Redeeming Relationships*, *Spiritual Fitness*, and *Communication Matters* and also codirects Redeemingrelationships.com

Together, Rich and Marty have spent several decades in churches and professional organizations helping couples strengthen their marriages. They welcome your insights on how to communicate these truths to the millions of Christians who want so desperately to lock on to the kind of love that is "stronger than death" (Song of Songs 8:6).

They encourage you to take advantage of the resources at Redeemingrelationships.com, including a free downloadable small group Bible study on Love Lock, and to contact them personally through the links posted there.